Principles to Actions

Ensuring Mathematical Success for All

NCTM

NATIONAL COUNCIL OF
TEACHERS OF MATHEMATICS

Copyright © 2014 by
The National Council of Teachers of Mathematics, Inc.
1906 Association Drive, Reston, VA 20191-1502
(703) 620-9840; (800) 235-7566; www.nctm.org
All rights reserved
Twelfth printing 2019

Library of Congress Cataloging-in-Publication Data

Principles to actions : ensuring mathematical success for all / writing
team, Steven Leinwand, American Institutes for Research [and 8 others].
    pages cm
  Includes bibliographical references.
  ISBN 978-0-87353-774-2
  1. Mathematics—Study and teaching—United States. 2. Effective
teaching. 3. Curriculum planning. I. National Council of Teachers of
Mathematics.
  QA13.P737 2014
  510.71'073—dc23
                        2014003343

The National Council of Teachers of Mathematics advocates for
high-quality mathematics teaching and learning for each and every student.

Principles to Actions: Ensuring Mathematical Success for All is an official position of the
National Council of Teachers of Mathematics as approved by the
NCTM Board of Directors, February 2014.

Printed in the United States of America

Contents

Principles to Actions
Writing Team

Steven Leinwand   **American Institutes for Research**
Washington, D.C.

Daniel J. Brahier   **Bowling Green State University**
Bowling Green, Ohio

DeAnn Huinker   **University of Wisconsin–Milwaukee**
Milwaukee, Wisconsin

Robert Q. Berry III   University of Virginia
Charlottesville, Virginia

Frederick L. Dillon   Strongsville City Schools (retired)
Strongsville, Ohio

Matthew R. Larson   Lincoln Public Schools
Lincoln, Nebraska

Miriam A. Leiva   University of North Carolina at Charlotte
Charlotte, North Carolina

W. Gary Martin   Auburn University
Auburn, Alabama

Margaret S. Smith   University of Pittsburgh
Pittsburgh, Pennsylvania

NCTM Board of Directors

Robert Q. Berry III	University of Virginia Charlottesville, Virginia
Margaret (Peg) Cagle	Vanderbilt University Nashville, Tennessee
Dane R. Camp	'Iolani School Honolulu, Hawaii
Mark W. Ellis	California State University, Fullerton Fullerton, California
Florence Glanfield	University of Alberta Edmonton, Alberta, Canada
Karen J. Graham	University of New Hampshire Durham, New Hampshire
Gladis Kersaint	University of South Florida Tampa, Florida
Latrenda Knighten	Polk Elementary School Baton Rouge, Louisiana
Ruth Harbin Miles	Falmouth Elementary School Mary Baldwin College Madison, Virginia
Jane Porath	Traverse City Area Public Schools Traverse City, Michigan
Jonathan (Jon) Wray	Howard County Public Schools Ellicott City, Maryland
Rose Mary Zbiek	The Pennsylvania State University University Park, Pennsylvania

Preface

The National Council of Teachers of Mathematics is proud to be the organization that launched the education standards movement. Growing out of its visionary *Agenda for Action* in 1980, NCTM's 1989 publication of *Curriculum and Evaluation Standards for School Mathematics* presented a comprehensive vision for mathematics teaching, learning, and assessment in kindergarten–grade 4, grades 5–8, and grades 9–12. In 2000, NCTM's *Principles and Standards for School Mathematics* expanded on the 1989 Standards and added underlying Principles for school mathematics for four grade bands: pre-K–grade 2, grades 3–5, grades 6–8, and grades 9–12. In 2006, *Curriculum Focal Points for Pre-kindergarten through Grade 8 Mathematics: A Quest for Coherence* extended this work by identifying the most significant mathematical concepts and skills at each level from prekindergarten through grade 8. NCTM addressed high school mathematics education in 2009 in *Focus in High School Mathematics: Reasoning and Sense Making.*

The next phase in the evolution of mathematics standards was the development of the Common Core State Standards for Mathematics by the National Governors Association and the Council of Chief State School Officers. The release of these standards in 2010, and their adoption by forty-five states, has presented a historic opportunity for mathematics education in the United States.

Over the past twenty-five years, we have learned that standards alone—no matter their origins, authorship, or the process by which they are developed—will not realize the goal of high levels of mathematical understanding by all students. More is needed than standards. For that reason, NCTM has developed *Principles to Actions: Ensuring Mathematical Success for All,* the next in its line of landmark publications guiding mathematics education into the future. *Principles to Actions* describes the conditions, structures, and policies that must exist for all students to learn. It addresses the essential elements of teaching and learning, access and equity, curriculum, tools and technology, assessment, and professionalism. Finally, it suggests specific actions that teachers and stakeholders need to take to realize our shared goal of ensuring mathematical success for all.

Principles to Actions represents a significant step in articulating a unified vision of what is needed to realize the potential of educating all students—under any standards or in any educational setting. Most important, it describes the actions required to ensure that all students learn to become mathematical thinkers and are prepared for any academic career or professional path that they choose. *Principles to Actions* is for teachers, coaches, specialists, principals, and other school leaders. It is for policymakers and leaders in districts and states, including commissioners, superintendents, and other central office administrators. Moreover, it will give families guidance about what to look for and expect in the system educating their children. *Principles to Actions* spells out the part that we all must play in supporting the success of today's students to ensure a bright future for the world around us.

Linda M. Gojak
President, 2012–2014
National Council of Teachers of Mathematics

Acknowledgments

The *Principles to Actions* Writing Team received many comments as a result of sharing the first draft with all members of the National Council of Teachers of Mathematics. The team also received and considered comments from a select group of invited reviewers. Some of these invited reviewers also read and commented on a second draft, which then underwent extensive further revisions before preparation of the final manuscript. Included among the reviewers were mathematicians, mathematics educators, curriculum developers, policymakers, and classroom practitioners. Several other individuals, committees, or groups committed to improving pre-K–12 mathematics teaching and learning offered their perceptions and comments less formally. The NCTM Board of Directors and the *Principles to Actions* Writing Team are grateful to all the reviewers who shared their expertise.

We extend sincere thanks to the following individuals who offered particularly thorough reviews or provided exceptional insights in sharing their perspectives on *Principles to Actions* in its formative stages. Their thoughtful contributions do not constitute endorsement of the final publication, but they provided the writing team with fresh perspectives that ultimately led to a better publication.

Cal Armstrong	Mark Ellis	Glenda Lappan
Don Balka	Francis (Skip) Fennell	Jim Lewis
Hyman Bass	Shirley Frye	Johnny Lott
Diane Briars	Karen Fuson	Susan Jo Russell
George Bright	Sol Garfunkel	Cathy Seeley
Gail Burrill	Martin Gartzman	J. Michael Shaughnessy
Margaret (Peg) Cagle	Patrick Hopfensberger	Linda Sheffield
Anne Collins	Andy Isaacs	Lee V. Stiff
Al Cuoco	Diana Kasbaum	Marilyn Strutchens
David Custer	Cathy Kelso	Denisse Thompson
Todd Davies	Henry S. Kepner, Jr.	Uri Treisman
Barbara Dougherty	Gladis Kersaint	Zalman Usiskin
Debbie Duvall	Michael Lach	Judith Zawojewski

NCTM and the *Principles to Actions* Writing Team also thank the *Mathematics Teacher* Editorial Panel and the Hoosier Association of Mathematics Teacher Educators for their collective thoughts and views, which helped to shape the work in progress and to refine the final publication.

Finally, special thanks go to the teachers and administration of Wheeler Elementary School in Louisville, Kentucky, whose work provided the basis for the illustration and student work that appear in the discussion of Assessment.

Progress and Challenge

I n 1989, the National Council of Teachers of Mathematics (NCTM) launched the standards-based education movement in North America with the release of *Curriculum and Evaluation Standards for School Mathematics*, an unprecedented initiative to promote systemic improvement in mathematics education. Now, twenty-five years later, the widespread adoption of college- and career-readiness standards, including adoption in the United States of the Common Core State Standards for Mathematics (CCSSM) by forty-five of the fifty states, provides an opportunity to reenergize and focus our commitment to significant improvement in mathematics education. To realize the potential of these new standards, we must examine the progress that has already been made, the challenges that remain, and the actions needed to truly ensure mathematical success for all students.

Looking back at mathematics education and student achievement in mathematics, we find much to celebrate. Owing in large measure to the leadership of NCTM, the gradual implementation of a growing body of research on teaching and learning mathematics, and the dedicated efforts of nearly two million teachers of mathematics in North America, student achievement is at historic highs:

- The percentage of fourth graders scoring "proficient" or above on the National Assessment of Educational Progress (NAEP) rose from 13 percent in 1990 to 42 percent in 2013. (National Center for Education Statistics [NCES] 2013)

- The percentage of eighth graders scoring "proficient" or above on the NAEP rose from 15 percent in 1990 to 36 percent in 2013. (NCES 2013)

- Average scores for fourth and eighth graders on these NAEP assessments rose 29 and 22 points, respectively, between 1990 and 2013. (NCES 2013)

- Between 1990 and 2013, the mean SAT-Math score increased from 501 to 514, and the mean ACT-Math score increased from 19.9 to 20.9. (College Board 2013a; ACT 2013)

- The number of students taking Advanced Placement Calculus examinations increased from 77,634 in 1982 to 387,297 in 2013, of whom about 50 percent scored 4 or 5. (College Board 2013b)

- The number of students taking the Advanced Placement Statistics examination increased from 7,667 in 1997 to 169,508 in 2013, of whom over 33 percent scored 4 or 5. (College Board 2013b)

These are impressive accomplishments. However, while we celebrate these record high NAEP scores and increases in SAT and ACT achievement—despite a significantly larger and more diverse range of test-takers—other recent data make it clear that we are far from where we need to be and that much still remains to be accomplished:

- Average mathematics NAEP scores for 17-year-olds have been essentially flat since 1973. (NCES 2009)

- The difference in average NAEP mathematics scores between white and black and white and Hispanic 9- and 13-year-olds has narrowed somewhat between 1973 and 2012 but remains between 17 and 28 points. (NCES 2013)

- Only about 44 percent of U.S. high school graduates in 2013 were considered ready for college work in mathematics, as measured by ACT and SAT scores. (ACT 2013; College Board 2013c)

- Among cohorts of 15-year-olds from the 34 countries participating in the 2012 Programme for International Student Assessment (PISA), which measures students' capacity to formulate, employ, and interpret mathematics in a variety of real-world contexts, the Canadian cohort ranked 13th in mathematics, placing it quite high among non–East Asian countries, whereas the U.S. cohort ranked 26th. (Organisation for Economic Co-operation and Development [OECD] 2013a)

- Although many countries' mean scores on the PISA assessments increased from 2003 to 2012, the United States' and Canada's mean scores declined. (OECD 2013a)

- U.S. students performed relatively well on PISA items that required only lower-level skills—reading and simple handling of data directly from tables and diagrams, handling easily manageable formulas—but they struggled with tasks involving creating, using, and interpreting models of real-world situations and using mathematical reasoning. (OECD 2013b)

- On the PISA tests, only 8.8 percent of students in the United States reached the top two mathematics levels, compared with 12.6 percent of the students across all 34 participating countries, including 16.4 percent of students in Canada and more than 30 percent of students in Hong Kong–China, Korea, Singapore, and Chinese Taipei. (OECD, 2013a)

- Only 16 percent of U.S. high school seniors are proficient in mathematics and interested in a STEM career. (U.S. Department of Education 2014).

These more disturbing data point to the persistent challenges and the work that we still need to do to make mathematics achievement a reality for all students:

- Eliminate persistent racial, ethnic, and income achievement gaps so that all students have opportunities and supports to achieve high levels of mathematics learning

- Increase the level of mathematics learning of all students, so that they are college and career ready when they graduate from high school

- Increase the number of high school graduates, especially those from traditionally underrepresented groups, who are interested in, and prepared for, STEM careers

In short, we must move from "pockets of excellence" to "systemic excellence" by providing mathematics education that supports the learning of all students at the highest possible level.

To achieve this goal, we must change a range of troubling and unproductive realities that exist in too many classrooms, schools, and districts. *Principles to Actions* discusses and documents these realities:

- Too much focus is on learning procedures without any connection to meaning, understanding, or the applications that require these procedures.

- Too many students are limited by the lower expectations and narrower curricula of remedial tracks from which few ever emerge.

- Too many teachers have limited access to the instructional materials, tools, and technology that they need.

- Too much weight is placed on results from assessments—particularly large-scale, high-stakes assessments—that emphasize skills and fact recall and fail to give sufficient attention to problem solving and reasoning.

- Too many teachers of mathematics remain professionally isolated, without the benefits of collaborative structures and coaching, and with inadequate opportunities for professional development related to mathematics teaching and learning.

As a result, too few students—especially those from traditionally underrepresented groups—are attaining high levels of mathematics learning.

Thus, this is no time to rest on laurels. Even a casual review of entry-level workplace expectations and the daily responsibilities of household management and citizenship suggest that such core mathematical ideas as proportion, rate of change, equality, dimension, random sample, and correlation must be understood by nearly all adults—a target far from the current reality.

What is different and promising today, however, is the hope that the implementation of CCSSM, and the new generation of aligned and rigorous assessments, will help to address the continuing challenges and expand the progress already made. The need for coherent standards that promote college and career readiness has been endorsed across all states and provinces, whether or not they have adopted CCSSM. As NCTM (2013) has publicly declared,

The widespread adoption of the Common Core State Standards for Mathematics presents an unprecedented opportunity for systemic improvement in mathematics education in the United States. The Common Core State Standards offer a foundation for the development of more rigorous, focused, and coherent mathematics curricula, instruction, and assessments that promote conceptual understanding and reasoning as well as skill fluency. This foundation will help to ensure that all students are ready for college and the workplace when they graduate from high school and that they are prepared to take their place as productive, full participants in society.

CCSSM provides guidance and direction, and helps focus and clarify common outcomes. It motivates the development of new instructional resources and assessments. But CCSSM does not tell teachers, coaches, administrators, parents, or policymakers what to do at the classroom, school, or district level or how to begin making essential changes to implement these standards. Moreover, it does not describe or prescribe the essential conditions required to ensure mathematical success for all students. Thus, the primary purpose of *Principles to Actions* is to fill this gap between the development and adoption of CCSSM and other standards and the enactment of practices, policies, programs, and actions required for their widespread and successful implementation. Its overarching message is that effective teaching is the nonnegotiable core that ensures that all students learn mathematics at high levels and that such teaching requires a range of actions at the state or provincial, district, school, and classroom levels.

In *Principles to Actions*, NCTM sets forth a set of strongly recommended, research-informed actions for all teachers, coaches, and specialists in mathematics; all school and district administrators; and all educational leaders and policymakers. These recommendations are based on the Council's core principles. In *Principles and Standards for School Mathematics*, NCTM (2000) first defined a set of Principles that "describe features of high-quality mathematics education" (p. 11). The list on the following page presents updated Principles that constitute the foundation of *Principles to Actions*.

The revisions to this updated set of Principles reflect more than a decade of experience and new research evidence about excellent mathematics programs, as well as significant obstacles and unproductive beliefs that continue to compromise progress. In succeeding sections, these six Principles are defined, examined for unproductive and productive beliefs, linked to effective practices, and illuminated with examples. The final section proposes specific actions for productive practices and policies that are essential for widespread implementation of pre-K–12 mathematics programs with the power to ensure mathematical success for all students at last.

Guiding Principles for School Mathematics

Teaching and Learning. An excellent mathematics program requires effective teaching that engages students in meaningful learning through individual and collaborative experiences that promote their ability to make sense of mathematical ideas and reason mathematically.

Access and Equity. An excellent mathematics program requires that all students have access to a high-quality mathematics curriculum, effective teaching and learning, high expectations, and the support and resources needed to maximize their learning potential.

Curriculum. An excellent mathematics program includes a curriculum that develops important mathematics along coherent learning progressions and develops connections among areas of mathematical study and between mathematics and the real world.

Tools and Technology. An excellent mathematics program integrates the use of mathematical tools and technology as essential resources to help students learn and make sense of mathematical ideas, reason mathematically, and communicate their mathematical thinking.

Assessment. An excellent mathematics program ensures that assessment is an integral part of instruction, provides evidence of proficiency with important mathematics content and practices, includes a variety of strategies and data sources, and informs feedback to students, instructional decisions, and program improvement.

Professionalism. In an excellent mathematics program, educators hold themselves and their colleagues accountable for the mathematical success of every student and for their personal and collective professional growth toward effective teaching and learning of mathematics.

Effective Teaching and Learning

An excellent mathematics program requires effective teaching that engages students in meaningful learning through individual and collaborative experiences that promote their ability to make sense of mathematical ideas and reason mathematically.

The teaching of mathematics is complex. It requires teachers to have a deep understanding of the mathematical knowledge that they are expected to teach (Ball, Thames, and Phelps 2008) and a clear view of how student learning of that mathematics develops and progresses across grades (Daro, Mosher, and Corcoran 2011; Sztajn et al. 2012). It also requires teachers to be skilled at teaching in ways that are effective in developing mathematics learning for all students. This section presents, describes, and illustrates a set of eight research-informed teaching practices that support the mathematics learning of all students. Before turning to these teaching practices, however, we must be clear about the mathematics learning such teaching must inspire and develop and the inextricable connection between teaching and learning.

The learning of mathematics has been defined to include the development of five interrelated strands that, together, constitute mathematical proficiency (National Research Council 2001):

1. Conceptual understanding

2. Procedural fluency

3. Strategic competence

4. Adaptive reasoning

5. Productive disposition

Conceptual understanding (i.e., the comprehension and connection of concepts, operations, and relations) establishes the foundation, and is necessary, for developing procedural fluency (i.e., the meaningful and flexible use of procedures to solve problems).

Strategic competence (i.e., the ability to formulate, represent, and solve mathematical problems) and adaptive reasoning (i.e., the capacity to think logically and to justify one's thinking) reflect the need for students to develop mathematical ways of thinking as a basis for solving mathematics problems that they may encounter in real life, as well as within mathematics and other disciplines. These ways of thinking are variously described as "processes" (in NCTM's [2000] Process Standards), "reasoning habits" (NCTM 2009), or "mathematical practices" (National Governors Association Center for Best Practices and Council of Chief State School Officers [NGA Center and CCSSO] 2010). In this publication, in alignment with the Common

Core State Standards for Mathematics (CCSSM), we refer to them as "mathematical practices," which represent what students are doing as they learn mathematics (see fig. 1).

1. Make sense of problems and persevere in solving them.

2. Reason abstractly and quantitatively.

3. Construct viable arguments and critique the reasoning of others.

4. Model with mathematics.

5. Use appropriate tools strategically.

6. Attend to precision.

7. Look for and make use of structure.

8. Look for and express regularity in repeated reasoning.

Fig. 1. Standards for Mathematical Practice (NGO Center and CCSSO 2010, pp. 6–8)

The fifth strand identified on the preceding page, productive disposition, is "the tendency to see sense in mathematics, to perceive it as both useful and worthwhile, to believe that steady effort in learning mathematics pays off, and to see oneself as an effective learner and doer of mathematics" (National Research Council 2001, p. 131). Students need to recognize the value of studying mathematics and believe that they are capable of learning mathematics through resolve and effort (Schunk and Richardson 2011). This conviction increases students' motivation and willingness to persevere in solving challenging problems in the short term and continuing their study of mathematics in the long term. Interest and curiosity evoked throughout the study of mathematics can spark a lifetime of positive attitudes toward the subject.

Student learning of mathematics "depends fundamentally on what happens inside the classroom as teachers and learners interact over the curriculum" (Ball and Forzani 2011, p. 17). Ball and other researchers (e.g., Ball et al. 2009; Grossman, Hammerness, and McDonald 2009; Lampert 2010; McDonald, Kazemi, and Kavanagh 2013) argue that the profession of teaching needs to identify and work together toward the implementation of a common set of high-leverage practices that underlie effective teaching. By "high-leverage practices," they mean "those practices at the heart of the work of teaching that are most likely to affect student learning" (Ball and Forzani 2010, p. 45).

Although effective teaching of mathematics may have similarities with productive teaching in other disciplines (Duit and Treagust 2003; Hlas and Hlas 2012), each discipline requires focused attention on those teaching practices that are most effective in supporting student learning specific to the discipline (Hill et al. 2008; Hill, Rowan, and Ball 2005). Research from both cognitive science (Mayer 2002; Bransford, Brown, and Cocking 2000; National

Research Council 2012a) and mathematics education (Donovan and Bransford 2005; Lester 2007) supports the characterization of mathematics learning as an active process, in which each student builds his or her own mathematical knowledge from personal experiences, coupled with feedback from peers, teachers and other adults, and themselves. This research has identified a number of principles of learning that provide the foundation for effective mathematics teaching. Specifically, learners should have experiences that enable them to—

- engage with challenging tasks that involve active meaning making and support meaningful learning;

- connect new learning with prior knowledge and informal reasoning and, in the process, address preconceptions and misconceptions;

- acquire conceptual knowledge as well as procedural knowledge, so that they can meaningfully organize their knowledge, acquire new knowledge, and transfer and apply knowledge to new situations;

- construct knowledge socially, through discourse, activity, and interaction related to meaningful problems;

- receive descriptive and timely feedback so that they can reflect on and revise their work, thinking, and understandings; and

- develop metacognitive awareness of themselves as learners, thinkers, and problem solvers, and learn to monitor their learning and performance.

Mathematics Teaching Practices

Eight Mathematics Teaching Practices provide a framework for strengthening the teaching and learning of mathematics. This research-informed framework of teaching and learning reflects the learning principles listed above, as well as other knowledge of mathematics teaching that has accumulated over the last two decades. The list on the following page identifies these eight Mathematics Teaching Practices, which represent a core set of high-leverage practices and essential teaching skills necessary to promote deep learning of mathematics.

Obstacles

Dominant cultural beliefs about the teaching and learning of mathematics continue to be obstacles to consistent implementation of effective teaching and learning in mathematics classrooms (Handal 2003; Philipp 2007). Many parents and educators believe that students should be taught as they were taught, through memorizing facts, formulas, and procedures and then practicing skills over and over again (e.g., Sam and Ernest 2000). This view perpetuates the traditional lesson paradigm that features review, demonstration, and practice and is still pervasive in many classrooms (Banilower et al. 2006; Weiss and Pasley 2004). Teachers, as well

Mathematics Teaching Practices
Establish mathematics goals to focus learning. Effective teaching of mathematics establishes clear goals for the mathematics that students are learning, situates goals within learning progressions, and uses the goals to guide instructional decisions.
Implement tasks that promote reasoning and problem solving. Effective teaching of mathematics engages students in solving and discussing tasks that promote mathematical reasoning and problem solving and allow multiple entry points and varied solution strategies.
Use and connect mathematical representations. Effective teaching of mathematics engages students in making connections among mathematical representations to deepen understanding of mathematics concepts and procedures and as tools for problem solving.
Facilitate meaningful mathematical discourse. Effective teaching of mathematics facilitates discourse among students to build shared understanding of mathematical ideas by analyzing and comparing student approaches and arguments.
Pose purposeful questions. Effective teaching of mathematics uses purposeful questions to assess and advance students' reasoning and sense making about important mathematical ideas and relationships.
Build procedural fluency from conceptual understanding. Effective teaching of mathematics builds fluency with procedures on a foundation of conceptual understanding so that students, over time, become skillful in using procedures flexibly as they solve contextual and mathematical problems.
Support productive struggle in learning mathematics. Effective teaching of mathematics consistently provides students, individually and collectively, with opportunities and supports to engage in productive struggle as they grapple with mathematical ideas and relationships.
Elicit and use evidence of student thinking. Effective teaching of mathematics uses evidence of student thinking to assess progress toward mathematical understanding and to adjust instruction continually in ways that support and extend learning.

as parents, are often not convinced that straying from these established beliefs and practices will be more effective for student learning (Barkatsas and Malone 2005; Wilken 2008).

In sharp contrast to this view is the belief that mathematics lessons should be centered on engaging students in solving and discussing tasks that promote reasoning and problem solving (NCTM 2009; National Research Council 2012a). Teachers who hold this belief plan lessons to prompt student interactions and discourse, with the goal of helping students make sense of mathematical concepts and procedures. However, the lack of agreement about what constitutes effective mathematics teaching constrains schools and school systems from establishing coherent expectations for high-quality, productive teaching of mathematics (Ball and Forzani 2011).

Teachers' beliefs influence the decisions that they make about the manner in which they teach mathematics, as indicated in the table at the right. Students' beliefs influence their

Beliefs about teaching and learning mathematics	
Unproductive beliefs	**Productive beliefs**
Mathematics learning should focus on practicing procedures and memorizing basic number combinations.	Mathematics learning should focus on developing understanding of concepts and procedures through problem solving, reasoning, and discourse.
Students need only to learn and use the same standard computational algorithms and the same prescribed methods to solve algebraic problems.	All students need to have a range of strategies and approaches from which to choose in solving problems, including, but not limited to, general methods, standard algorithms, and procedures.
Students can learn to apply mathematics only after they have mastered the basic skills.	Students can learn mathematics through exploring and solving contextual and mathematical problems.
The role of the teacher is to tell students exactly what definitions, formulas, and rules they should know and demonstrate how to use this information to solve mathematics problems.	The role of the teacher is to engage students in tasks that promote reasoning and problem solving and facilitate discourse that moves students toward shared understanding of mathematics.
The role of the student is to memorize information that is presented and then use it to solve routine problems on homework, quizzes, and tests.	The role of the student is to be actively involved in making sense of mathematics tasks by using varied strategies and representations, justifying solutions, making connections to prior knowledge or familiar contexts and experiences, and considering the reasoning of others.
An effective teacher makes the mathematics easy for students by guiding them step by step through problem solving to ensure that they are not frustrated or confused.	An effective teacher provides students with appropriate challenge, encourages perseverance in solving problems, and supports productive struggle in learning mathematics.

perception of what it means to learn mathematics and their dispositions toward the subject. As the table summarizes, the impact of these beliefs on the teaching and learning of mathematics may be unproductive or productive. It is important to note that these beliefs should not be viewed as good or bad. Instead, beliefs should be understood as unproductive when they hinder the implementation of effective instructional practice or limit student access to important mathematics content and practices.

Overcoming the obstacles

Teaching mathematics requires specialized expertise and professional knowledge that includes not only knowing mathematics but knowing it in ways that make it useful for the work of teaching (Ball and Forzani 2010; Ball, Thames, and Phelps 2008). Mathematics teaching demands subject-specific understanding and insight so that teachers can skillfully carry out their work in mathematics classrooms. Some of the work of mathematics teaching includes finding an example or task to make a specific mathematical point, linking mathematical representations to underlying ideas and other representations, and evaluating students' mathematical reasoning and explanations. This work also requires teachers to be able to unpack mathematical topics that they know well and to reexamine these through the eyes of learners, as well as to be able to work with many learners simultaneously in classrooms, each with unique backgrounds, interests, and learning needs.

The following discussion and illustrations of the eight Mathematics Teaching Practices support the incorporation of the productive beliefs identified above into the daily professional work of effective teachers of mathematics. This framework offers educators within schools and across districts a common lens for collectively moving toward improved instructional practice and for supporting one another in becoming skilled at teaching in ways that matter for ensuring successful mathematics learning for all students.

Establish Mathematics Goals to Focus Learning

Effective teaching of mathematics establishes clear goals for the mathematics that students are learning, situates goals within learning progressions, and uses the goals to guide instructional decisions.

Effective mathematics teaching begins with a shared understanding among teachers of the mathematics that students are learning and how this mathematics develops along learning progressions. This shared understanding includes clarifying the broader mathematical goals that guide planning on a unit-by-unit basis, as well as the more targeted mathematics goals that guide instructional decisions on a lesson-by-lesson basis. The establishment of clear goals not only guides teachers' decision making during a lesson but also focuses students' attention on monitoring their own progress toward the intended learning outcomes.

Discussion

Mathematics goals indicate what mathematics students are to learn and understand as a result of instruction (Wiliam 2011). In fact, "formulating clear, explicit learning goals sets the stage for everything else" (Hiebert et al. 2007, p. 57). Goals should describe what mathematical concepts, ideas, or methods students will understand more deeply as a result of instruction and identify the mathematical practices that students are learning to use more proficiently. Teachers need to be clear about how the learning goals relate to and build toward rigorous standards, such as the Common Core State Standards for Mathematics. The goals that guide instruction, however, should not be just a reiteration of a standard statement or cluster but should be more specifically linked to the current classroom curriculum and student learning needs, referring, for example, to particular visual representations or mathematical concepts and methods that students will come to understand as a result of instruction.

Learning goals situated within mathematics learning progressions (Daro, Mosher, and Corcoran 2011) and connected to the "big ideas" of mathematics (Charles 2005) provide a stronger basis for teachers' instructional decisions. Learning progressions or trajectories describe how students make transitions from their prior knowledge to more sophisticated understandings. The progressions also identify intermediate understandings and link research on student learning to instruction (Clements and Sarama 2004; Sztajn et al. 2012). Both teachers and students need to be able to answer crucial questions:

- What mathematics is being learned?
- Why is it important?
- How does it relate to what has already been learned?
- Where are these mathematical ideas going?

Situating learning goals within the mathematical landscape supports opportunities to build explicit connections so that students see how ideas build on and relate to one another and come to view mathematics as a coherent and connected discipline (Fosnot and Jacob 2010; Ma 2010).

The mathematical purpose of a lesson should not be a mystery to students. Classrooms in which students understand the learning expectations for their work perform at higher levels than classrooms where the expectations are unclear (Haystead and Marzano 2009; Hattie 2009). Although daily goals need not be posted, it is important that students understand the mathematical purpose of a lesson and how the activities contribute to and support their mathematics learning. Goals or essential questions motivate learning when students perceive the goals as challenging but attainable (Marzano 2003; McTighe and Wiggins 2013). Teachers can discuss student-friendly versions of the mathematics goals as appropriate during the lesson so that students see value in and understand the purpose of their work (Black and Wiliam 1998a; Marzano 2009). When teachers refer to the goals during instruction, students become more focused and better able to perform self-assessment and monitor their own learning (Clarke, Timperley, and Hattie 2004; Zimmerman 2001).

A clear grasp of the mathematics frames the decisions that teachers make as they plan mathematics lessons, make adjustments during instruction, and reflect after instruction on the progress that students are making toward the goals. In particular, by establishing specific goals and considering how they connect with the broader mathematical landscape, teachers are better prepared to use the goals to make decisions during instruction (Hiebert et al. 2007). This includes facilitating meaningful discourse, ensuring connections among mathematical ideas, supporting students as they struggle, and determining what counts as evidence of students' learning (Seidle, Rimmele, and Prenzel, 2005). The practice of establishing clear goals that indicate what mathematics students are learning provides the starting point and foundation for intentional and effective teaching.

Illustration

Establishing clear goals begins with clarifying and understanding the mathematical expectations for student learning. Figure 2 presents an excerpt from a session in which two teachers, Ms. Burke and Mr. Miller, together with their math coach, engage in a collaborative planning session to discuss and clarify the mathematics learning goals for their second-grade students. Notice how the teachers begin by describing what the students will be doing in the lesson, rather than what they will be learning. Of course, teachers need to attend to the logistics of a lesson, but they must also give sufficient attention to establishing a detailed understanding of the mathematics learning goals. Consider how the math coach intentionally shifts the conversation to a discussion of the mathematical ideas and learning that will be the focus of instruction.

Two classes of second-grade students are currently working on understanding and solving addition and subtraction problems set in real-world situations. The following conversation develops among two teachers and their math coach in a planning session. The teachers have selected three story problems to give meaning to subtraction and serve as a focus for one of the lessons:

- Morgan wants to buy the next book in her favorite series when it is released next month. So far, she has saved $15. The book will cost $22. How much more money does Morgan need to save so that she can buy the book? (Problem type: Add to/ Change Unknown)

- George and his dad are in charge of blowing up balloons for the party. The package had 36 balloons in it. After blowing up many balloons, George's dad noticed that the package still contained 9 balloons. How many balloons had they blown up? (Problem type: Take from/Change Unknown)

- Lou and Natalie are preparing to run a marathon. Lou ran 43 training miles this week. Natalie ran 27 miles. How much farther did Lou run than Natalie? (Problem type: Compare/Difference Unknown)

Ms. Burke:	I think we should have the students work together in small groups to solve the word problems.
Mr. Miller:	I agree, and they could take turns reading the problems, and then everyone could draw diagrams or use cubes to solve them, and then they could compare their answers.

Fig. 2. Collaborative planning session focused on clarifying mathematics goals for a lesson on problem situations for subtraction

Math Coach:	OK, that's what you want the students to do. So now let's talk more about what is it that you want your students to learn as a result of this lesson.
Ms. Burke:	We want them to better understand these different types of word problems and be able to solve them.
Math Coach:	OK. So, let's list some of the indicators that would show they understand.
Mr. Miller:	They would be able to use cubes or draw diagrams to show what is happening in the problem, explain what they did and why, and be able to get the right answer.
Ms. Burke:	I also want them to write an equation that models each situation. Some of the equations might be $15 + \square = 22$, $36 = \square + 9$ or $36 - \square = 9$, and $43 - 27 = \square$ or $43 = 27 + \square$.
Mr. Miller:	Then if we have time in this lesson, or maybe the next day, we want the students to compare the different problems and equations and be able to explain how these relate to addition and subtraction, even though the contexts seem so different.
Math Coach:	Can you say a little more about why you picked these three problems for this lesson?
Mr. Miller:	Each word problem is about a different situation that gives meaning to subtraction. One problem is about finding an unknown addend, one is about subtraction as taking away, and the other is about finding the difference when comparing two amounts.
Ms. Burke:	We are hoping that the students get better at thinking about the relationships among the quantities in each context and how this relates to addition and subtraction. And they need to be able to work with these harder problem types and not just the easy take-away word problems [*i.e., Take from/Result Unknown*].
Math Coach:	Let me see if I can summarize this for us. Your learning goals for these lessons are for the students to represent and solve word problems by using diagrams or objects and equations, compare how the problem situations are similar and different, and explain how the underlying structure in each problem relates to addition and subtraction.
Ms. Burke:	Yes, and in their explanations, I want to hear them talk about what each number means in the problem, so in this lesson they know the total amount and one of the parts or addends, and they need to find the other unknown addend.

Note: Classification of problem types is based on CCSSM Glossary, Table 1 (NGA Center and CCSSO 2010, p. 88).

Fig. 2. *Continued*

As a result of the planning conversation, the teachers have a more precise understanding of the addition and subtraction concepts that they hope will surface during the lesson. For example, they expect their students to connect math drawings and equations and compare the mathematical structures of the various types of problem situations. At the beginning of the lesson, they discuss with students the goal and importance of understanding different kinds of word problems by using math drawings and writing equations. During instruction, the teachers are attentive to ensuring that students are not just finding the answers to the word problems but are able to explain how each problem relates to addition and subtraction and how that relationship is reflected in their drawings and equations. This in turn will compel students to focus on the how these problem situations relate to addition and subtraction and why that is an important aspect in their learning of mathematics.

Teacher and student actions

Effective teaching requires a clear understanding of what students need to accomplish mathematically. Clear learning goals focus the work of teaching and student learning. Teachers need to establish clear and detailed goals that indicate what mathematics students are learning, and they need to use these goals to guide decision making during instruction. Students also need to understand the mathematical purpose of a lesson. Teachers should help students understand how specific activities contribute to and support the students' learning of mathematics as appropriate during instruction. Students can then gauge and monitor their own learning progress. The actions listed in the table below provide guidance on what teachers and students do in establishing and using goals to focus learning in the mathematics classroom.

Establish mathematics goals to focus learning Teacher and student actions	
What are *teachers* doing?	**What are *students* doing?**
Establishing clear goals that articulate the mathematics that students are learning as a result of instruction in a lesson, over a series of lessons, or throughout a unit.	Engaging in discussions of the mathematical purpose and goals related to their current work in the mathematics classroom (e.g., What are we learning? Why are we learning it?)
Identifying how the goals fit within a mathematics learning progression.	Using the learning goals to stay focused on their progress in improving their understanding of mathematics content and proficiency in using mathematical practices.
Discussing and referring to the mathematical purpose and goal of a lesson during instruction to ensure that students understand how the current work contributes to their learning.	Connecting their current work with the mathematics that they studied previously and seeing where the mathematics is going.
Using the mathematics goals to guide lesson planning and reflection and to make in-the-moment decisions during instruction.	Assessing and monitoring their own understanding and progress toward the mathematics learning goals.

Implement Tasks That Promote Reasoning and Problem Solving

Effective teaching of mathematics engages students in solving and discussing tasks that promote mathematical reasoning and problem solving and allow multiple entry points and varied solution strategies.

Effective mathematics teaching uses tasks as one way to motivate student learning and help students build new mathematical knowledge through problems solving. Research on the use of mathematical tasks over the last two decades has yielded three major findings:

1. Not all tasks provide the same opportunities for student thinking and learning. (Hiebert et al. 1997; Stein et al. 2009)

2. Student learning is greatest in classrooms where the tasks consistently encourage high-level student thinking and reasoning and least in classrooms where the tasks are routinely procedural in nature. (Boaler and Staples 2008; Hiebert and Wearne 1993; Stein and Lane 1996)

3. Tasks with high cognitive demands are the most difficult to implement well and are often transformed into less demanding tasks during instruction. (Stein, Grover, and Henningsen 1996; Stigler and Hiebert 2004)

To ensure that students have the opportunity to engage in high-level thinking, teachers must regularly select and implement tasks that promote reasoning and problem solving. These tasks encourage reasoning and access to the mathematics through multiple entry points, including the use of different representations and tools, and they foster the solving of problems through varied solution strategies.

Furthermore, effective teachers understand how contexts, culture, conditions, and language can be used to create mathematical tasks that draw on students' prior knowledge and experiences (Cross et al. 2012; Kisker et. al. 2012; Moschkovich 1999, 2011) or that offer students a common experience from which their work on mathematical tasks emerges (Boaler 1997; Dubinsky and Wilson 2013; Wager 2012). As a result of teachers' efforts to incorporate these elements into mathematical tasks, students' engagement in solving these tasks is more strongly connected with their sense of identity, leading to increased engagement and motivation in mathematics (Aguirre, Mayfield-Ingram, and Martin 2013; Boaler 1997; Hogan 2008; Middleton and Jansen 2011).

Discussion

Mathematical tasks can range from a set of routine exercises to a complex and challenging problem that focuses students' attention on a particular mathematical idea. Stein and colleagues

(Stein, Grover, and Henningsen 1996; Stein and Smith 1998) have developed a taxonomy of mathematical tasks based on the kind and level of thinking required to solve them. Smith and Stein (1998) show the characteristics of higher- and lower-level tasks and provide samples in each category; figure 3 reproduces their list of the characteristics of tasks at four levels of cognitive demand, and figure 4 provides examples of tasks at each of the levels.

Levels of Demands

Lower-level demands (memorization):
- Involve either reproducing previously learned facts, rules, formulas, or definitions or committing facts, rules, formulas or definitions to memory
- Cannot be solved using procedures because a procedure does not exist or because the time frame in which the task is being completed is too short to use a procedure
- Are not ambiguous. Such tasks involve the exact reproduction of previously seen material, and what is to be reproduced is clearly and directly stated.
- Have no connection to the concepts or meaning that underlie the facts, rules, formulas, or definitions being learned or reproduced

Lower-level demands (procedures without connections):
- Are algorithmic. Use of the procedure either is specifically called for or is evident from prior instruction, experience, or placement of the task.
- Require limited cognitive demand for successful completion. Little ambiguity exists about what needs to be done and how to do it.
- Have no connection to the concepts or meaning that underlie the procedure being used
- Are focused on producing correct answers instead of on developing mathematical understanding
- Require no explanations or explanations that focus solely on describing the procedure that was used

Higher-level demands (procedures with connections):
- Focus students' attention on the use of procedures for the purpose of developing deeper levels of understanding of mathematical concepts and ideas
- Suggest explicitly or implicitly pathways to follow that are broad general procedures that have close connections to underlying conceptual ideas as opposed to narrow algorithms that are opaque with respect to underlying concepts
- Usually are represented in multiple ways, such as visual diagrams, manipulatives, symbols, and problem situations. Making connections among multiple representations helps develop meaning.
- Require some degree of cognitive effort. Although general procedures may be followed, they cannot be followed mindlessly. Students need to engage with conceptual ideas that underlie the procedures to complete the task successfully and that develop understanding.

Higher-level demands (doing mathematics):
- Require complex and nonalgorithmic thinking—a predictable, well-rehearsed approach or pathway is not explicitly suggested by the task, task instructions, or a worked-out example.
- Require students to explore and understand the nature of mathematical concepts, processes, or relationships
- Demand self-monitoring or self-regulation of one's own cognitive processes
- Require students to access relevant knowledge and experiences and make appropriate use of them in working through the task
- Require students to analyze the task and actively examine task constraints that may limit possible solution strategies and solutions
- Require considerable cognitive effort and may involve some level of anxiety for the student because of the unpredictable nature of the solution process required

These characteristics are derived from the work of Doyle on academic tasks (1988) and Resnick on high-level-thinking skills (1987), the *Professional Standards for Teaching Mathematics* (NCTM 1991), and the examination and categorization of hundreds of tasks used in QUASAR classrooms (Stein, Grover, and Henningsen 1996; Stein, Lane, and Silver 1996).

Fig. 3. Characteristics of mathematical tasks at four levels of cognitive demand. From Smith and Stein (1998).

Lower-Level Demands

Memorization

What is the rule for multiplying fractions?

Expected student response:

You multiply the numerator times the numerator and the denominator times the denominator.

or

You multiply the two top numbers and then the two bottom numbers.

Procedures without Connections

Multiply:

$$\frac{2}{3} \times \frac{3}{4}$$

$$\frac{5}{6} \times \frac{7}{8}$$

$$\frac{4}{9} \times \frac{3}{5}$$

Expected student response:

$$\frac{2}{3} \times \frac{3}{4} = \frac{2 \times 3}{3 \times 4} = \frac{6}{12}$$

$$\frac{5}{6} \times \frac{7}{8} = \frac{5 \times 7}{6 \times 8} = \frac{35}{48}$$

$$\frac{4}{9} \times \frac{3}{5} = \frac{4 \times 3}{9 \times 5} = \frac{12}{45}$$

Higher-Level Demands

Procedures with Connections

Find 1/6 of 1/2. Use pattern blocks. Draw your answer and explain your solution.

Expected student response:

First you take half of the whole, which would be one hexagon. Then you take one-sixth of that half. So I divided the hexagon into six pieces, which would be six triangles. I only needed one-sixth, so that would be one triangle. Then I needed to figure out what part of the two hexagons one triangle was, and it was 1 out of 12. So 1/6 of 1/2 is 1/12.

Doing Mathematics

Create a real-world situation for the following problem:

$$\frac{2}{3} \times \frac{3}{4}.$$

Solve the problem you have created without using the rule, and explain your solution.

One possible student response:

For lunch Mom gave me three-fourths of a pizza that we ordered. I could only finish two-thirds of what she gave me. How much of the whole pizza did I eat?

I drew a rectangle to show the whole pizza. Then I cut it into fourths and shaded three of them to show the part Mom gave me. Since I only ate two-thirds of what she gave me, that would be only two of the shaded sections.

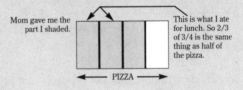

Mom gave me the part I shaded.

This is what I ate for lunch. So 2/3 of 3/4 is the same thing as half of the pizza.

◄— PIZZA —►

Fig. 4. Sample tasks for four levels of cognitive demand. From Smith and Stein (1998).

From the perspective of this taxonomy, mathematical tasks are viewed as placing *higher-level* cognitive demands on students when they allow students to engage in active inquiry and exploration or encourage students to use procedures in ways that are meaningfully connected with concepts or understanding. Tasks that encourage students to use procedures, formulas, or algorithms in ways that are not actively linked to meaning, or that consist primarily of memorization or the reproduction of previously memorized facts, are viewed as placing *lower-level* cognitive demands on students. Consider figure 5, which shows two tasks, both of which might be used in an algebra unit that includes analyzing and solving pairs of simultaneous equations.

Task A: Smartphone Plans	Task B: Solving systems of equations
You are trying to decide which of two smartphone plans would be better. Plan A charges a basic fee of $30 per month and 10 cents per text message. Plan B charges a basic fee of $50 per month and 5 cents per text message. How many text messages would you need to send per month for plan B to be the better option? Explain your decision. (Adapted from Illustrative Mathematics Illustrations: www.illustrativemathematics.org/illustrations/469.)	Solve each of the following systems: $-4x - 2y = -12$ $4x + 8y = -24$ $x - y = 11$ $2x + y = 19$ $8x + y = -1$ $-3x + y = -5$ $5x + y = 9$ $10x - 7y = -18$

Fig. 5. Comparison of tasks with different cognitive demand

Task A is a high-level task, since no specific pathway has been suggested or is implied, and students could use several different approaches to enter and solve the task (e.g., guess and check, make a table, graph equations to find the point of intersection, solve a system of two linear equations by using algebra). Further, students must put forth effort to determine and enact a course of action and justify the reasonableness and accuracy of their solutions. By contrast, task B is a low-level task because it is likely that students are expected to use a specific memorized procedure that leaves little or no ambiguity about what they need to do. The mathematics that students can learn in doing a high-level task is significantly different from the mathematics that they learn from low-level tasks. Over time, the cumulative effect of the use of mathematics tasks is students' implicit development of ideas about the nature of mathematics—about whether mathematics is something that they personally can make sense of and how long and how hard they should have to work to solve any mathematical task.

It is important to note that not all tasks that promote reasoning and problem solving have to be set in a context or need to consume an entire class period or multiple days. What is critical is that a task provide students with the opportunity to engage actively in reasoning, sense making, and problem solving so that they develop a deep understanding of mathematics. Take, for example, the task on exponential functions in figure 6, which calls on students to analyze functions by using visual representations. In working on this task, students explore what happens to the graph of the function when the values of a change, and through their use of representations, they generalize the behavior of the function.

Using your graphing calculator, investigate the changes that occur in the graph of $y = a^x$ for different values of a, where a is any real number. Explain what happens in the following cases:

(1) $a > 1$

(2) $a = 1$

(3) $0 < a < 1$

(4) $a = 0$

(5) $a < 0$

Fig. 6. An algebra task requiring students to use graphical representations to analyze exponential functions

This task promotes problem solving because students are positioned to explore the situation without being told in advance what to expect. Through reasoning about this task, they are likely to determine the general shape of the graph of the function (e.g., when $a > 1$, the graph starts out "flat" and close to the x-axis and then shoots up; when $0 < a < 1$, the graph shows a rapidly shrinking function), what occurs at 0 and 1, and the difference between a growth function and a decay function. Extending this discussion to the case of $a < 0$ provides an important opportunity for students to learn why exponential functions are restricted to $a \geq 0$.

Tasks engaging students in reasoning and problem solving are not limited to middle and high school content. Consider the task in figure 7, in which students in kindergarten–grade 1 decompose the number 10 into pairs in more than one way.

There are 10 cars in the parking lot. Some of the cars are red and some of the cars are black. How many red cars and how many black cars could be in the parking lot?

Think of as many different combinations of cars as you can.

Show your solutions in as many ways as you can with cubes, drawings, or words, and write an equation for each solution.

Fig. 7. A task for K–grade 1 on number pairs that make 10. Adapted from the North Carolina Department of Public Instruction; http://commoncoretasks.ncdpi.wikispaces.net/First+Grade+Tasks.

In this problem, students identify one or more combinations that equal 10, using drawings, cubes, or other tools (e.g., fingers, ten frame, Rekenrek) as needed to support their problem solving and explaining. This is a high-level task for most kindergarten and first-grade students because they have not yet learned these combinations, and they can use a variety of strategies (e.g., trial and error, counting up to 10 from a selected number, decomposing 10 into two sets) to determine the combinations that will work. Through the process of solving this task, students may recognize similar combinations (e.g., $4 + 6 = 6 + 4$) and begin to see number patterns (e.g., $1 + 9$, $2 + 8$, $3 + 7$; as one number gets bigger by 1, the other number gets smaller by 1).

In determining the level of task, it is important to consider the prior knowledge and experiences of the students who will be engaged in the task. Tasks may begin as high-level tasks for students who are initially learning about the underlying mathematics (e.g., systems of linear equations, behaviors of functions, number combinations). Eventually, as students solidify their understanding of the underlying mathematics, these tasks may become more routine experiences for them. Students then need tasks that further extend these mathematical ideas in ways that continue to deepen understanding and strengthen mathematical reasoning and problem solving.

Illustration

Although selecting tasks that promote reasoning and problem solving is a critical first step, giving the task to students does not guarantee that students will actually engage in the task at a high level. Consider the comparison that figure 8 presents in the implementation of task A, Smartphone Plans, shown in figure 5, in two algebra classrooms.

Note that although Ms. Carson uses a task that could promote reasoning, as soon as she sees students struggling, she provides them with a pathway for solving the task. By taking over the thinking for her students, Ms. Carson removes their opportunity to engage deeply and meaningfully with the mathematics and leaves them simply to apply a specific procedure.

By contrast, when Ms. McDonald sees her students struggling to figure out what to do, she provides suggestions that will help them make progress on the task without giving them a specific pathway to follow. This is the approach that NCTM (2000 p. 19) has long advocated:

> Teachers must decide what aspects of a task to highlight, how to organize and orchestrate the work of the students, what questions to ask to challenge those with varied levels of expertise, and how to support students without taking over the process of thinking for them and thus eliminating the challenge.

As a result of the way in which Ms. McDonald orchestrates the lesson, students have the opportunity to consider different strategies and engage in mathematical problem solving at a

As students in two algebra classrooms begin working with their partners on the Smartphone Plans task, it becomes evident that students are struggling to get started.

Ms. Carson's classroom

Ms. Carson calls the class together and tells the students that they first need to write equations for both smartphone plans. She writes $y = mx + b$ on the board and asks students what m and b would be for each phone plan. Once they have established the two equations, she goes to the board and creates a table that contains three columns: x (number of text messages), y_1 (cost for plan A), and y_2 (cost for plan B). She suggests that they begin with 0 text messages and then increment the x values in the table by 10. The students resume their work with their partners and easily complete the table, identifying (400, 70) as the point of intersection of the two equations.

Ms. McDonald's classroom

Ms. McDonald poses questions to students as she walks around the room. When she notices students struggling to get started, she asks them how much it will cost to send one text message in each plan. This question enables her to be sure that the students understand the relationship among the number of messages, the cost per message, and the basic fee. She asks them which plan will cost more for a specific number of messages and to consider whether this plan's cost will always be higher. Then she leaves the partners to discuss ways to use this information to solve the problem. As the students continue working, she observes different approaches, hears debates on whether the answer is 400 messages or 401 messages, and plans how to sequence the whole-class discussion to analyze and compare the varied strategies.

Fig. 8. A look inside two algebra classrooms at the implementation of Smartphone Plans (task A in fig. 5)

high level of cognitive demand. Moreover, and most important, the students are challenged to deepen their understanding of linear equations and what the point of intersection means, both graphically and contextually.

Teacher and student actions

For students to learn mathematics with understanding, they must have opportunities to engage on a regular basis with tasks that focus on reasoning and problem solving and make possible multiple entry points and varied solution strategies. The actions listed in the table on the next page provide a summary of what teachers and students need to do when implementing such tasks in the mathematics classroom. It is important to note that tasks that focus on learning and applying procedures do have a place in the curriculum and are necessary for developing fluency. Such tasks, however, should not dominate instruction and preempt the use of tasks that promote reasoning. Instead, these tasks should build on and emerge from these sense-making and problem-solving experiences.

Implement tasks that promote reasoning and problem solving Teacher and student actions	
What are *teachers* doing?	What are *students* doing?
Motivating students' learning of mathematics through opportunities for exploring and solving problems that build on and extend their current mathematical understanding.	Persevering in exploring and reasoning through tasks.
Selecting tasks that provide multiple entry points through the use of varied tools and representations.	Taking responsibility for making sense of tasks by drawing on and making connections with their prior understanding and ideas.
Posing tasks on a regular basis that require a high level of cognitive demand.	Using tools and representations as needed to support their thinking and problem solving.
Supporting students in exploring tasks without taking over student thinking.	Accepting and expecting that their classmates will use a variety of solution approaches and that they will discuss and justify their strategies to one another.
Encouraging students to use varied approaches and strategies to make sense of and solve tasks.	

Use and Connect Mathematical Representations

Effective teaching of mathematics engages students in making connections among mathematical representations to deepen understanding of mathematics concepts and procedures and as tools for problem solving.

Effective mathematics teaching includes a strong focus on using varied mathematical representations. NCTM (2000) highlighted the important role of mathematical representations in the teaching and learning of mathematics by including the Process Standard for Representation in *Principles and Standards for School Mathematics*. Representations embody critical features of mathematical constructs and actions, such as drawing diagrams and using words to show and explain the meaning of fractions, ratios, or the operation of multiplication. When students learn to represent, discuss, and make connections among mathematical ideas in multiple forms, they demonstrate deeper mathematical understanding and enhanced problem-solving abilities (Fuson, Kalchman, and Bransford 2005; Lesh, Post, and Behr 1987).

Discussion

The general classification scheme for types of representations shown in figure 9 indicates important connections among contextual, visual, verbal, physical, and symbolic representational forms (Lesh, Post, and Behr 1987). Tripathi (2008) noted that using these "different representations is like examining the concept through a variety of lenses, with each lens providing a different perspective that makes the picture (concept) richer and deeper" (p. 439). Students, especially young learners, also benefit from using physical objects or acting out processes during problem solving (National Research Council 2009).

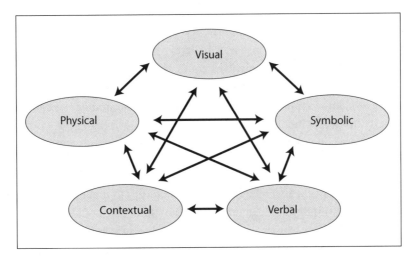

Fig. 9. Important connections among mathematical representations

According to the National Research Council (2001), "Because of the abstract nature of mathematics, people have access to mathematical ideas only through the representations of those ideas" (p. 94). The depth of understanding is related to the strength of connections among mathematical representations that students have internalized (Pape and Tchoshanov 2001; Webb, Boswinkel, and Dekker 2008). For example, students develop understanding of the meaning of the fraction $7/4$ (symbolic form) when they can see it as the quantity formed by "7 parts of size one-fourth" with a tape diagram or on a number line (visual form), or measure a string that has a length of 7-fourths yards (physical form).

Visual representations are of particular importance in the mathematics classroom, helping students to advance their understanding of mathematical concepts and procedures, make sense of problems, and engage in mathematical discourse (Arcavi 2003; Stylianou and Silver 2004). Visuals support problem solving as students consider relationships among quantities when they sketch diagrams or make tables and graphs. The visual representations also support discourse because the diagrams or drawings leave a trace of student problem solving that can be displayed, critiqued, and discussed. Math drawings and other visual supports are of particular importance for English language learners, learners with special needs, or struggling learners, because they allow more students to participate meaningfully in the mathematical discourse in the classroom (Fuson and Murata 2007). The visuals assist students in following the reasoning of their classmates and in giving voice to their own explanations as they gesture to parts of their math drawings and other visual representations.

Students' understanding is deepened through discussion of similarities among representations that reveal underlying mathematical structures or essential features of mathematical ideas that persist regardless of the form (Zimba 2011). For example, fractions are composed of the iteration of unit fractions, a structure that can be identified and discussed when students use paper strips as fraction models, draw tape diagrams or number lines, or use symbols. Likewise, the addition of fractions has a structure that is similar to that of the addition of whole numbers, in that all addition involves combining same-sized units, such as adding tens to tens or twelfths to twelfths. Mathematical structure can also be emphasized and discussed by asking students to translate or alternate directionality among the various representations, such as by linking symbols back to contexts (e.g., describing a real-world situation for 3×29 or $y = 3x + 5$), making a table of values for a given ratio, or making a graph based on the information in a table (Greeno and Hall 1997).

Success in solving problems is also related to students' ability to move flexibly among representations (Huinker 2013; Stylianou and Silver 2004). Students should be able to approach a problem from several points of view and be encouraged to switch among representations until they are able to understand the situation and proceed along a path that will lead them to a solution. This implies that students view representations as tools that they can use to help them solve problems, rather than as an end in themselves. If, by contrast, algebra tiles or base-ten blocks, for instance, are not used meaningfully, students may view use of the physical objects as the goal instead of reaching an understanding of how the tiles allow them to make sense of polynomials or how the base-ten blocks show the structure of the base-ten number system.

Illustration

Students' representational competence can be developed through instruction. Marshall, Superfine, and Canty (2010, p. 40) suggest three specific strategies:

1. Encourage purposeful selection of representations.
2. Engage in dialogue about explicit connections among representations.
3. Alternate the direction of the connections made among representations.

Consider the lesson presented in figure 10, and focus on how the teacher, Mr. Harris, uses these strategies with his third-grade students as they represent and solve a problem involving setting up chairs for a band concert.

The third-grade class is responsible for setting up the chairs for the spring band concert. In preparation, they have to determine the total number of chairs that will be needed and ask the school's engineer to retrieve that many chairs from the central storage area.

Mr. Harris explains to his students that they need to set up 7 rows of chairs with 20 chairs in each row, leaving space for a center aisle. Next he asks the students to consider how they might represent the problem: "Before you begin working on the task, think about a representation you might want to use and why, and then turn and share your ideas with a partner."

The students then set to work on the task. Most sketch equal groups or decompose area models. Two students cut an array out of grid paper. A few students make a table or T-chart, listing the number of rows with the corresponding number of chairs. Some students use symbolic approaches, such as repeated addition or partial products.

A few students change representations as they work. Dominique starts to draw tally marks but then switches to using a table. When Mr. Harris asks her why, she explains that she got tired of making all those marks. Similarly, Jamal starts to build an array with connecting cubes but then switches to drawing an array. These initial attempts are valuable, if not essential, in helping each of these students make sense of the situation.

As the students work, the teacher poses purposeful questions to press them to consider critical features of their representations: "How does your drawing show 7 groups?" "Why are you adding all those twenties?" "How many twenties are you adding, and why?"

Before holding a whole-class discussion, Mr. Harris has the students find a classmate who used a different representation and directs them to take turns explaining and comparing their work as well as their solutions. For example, Jasmine, who drew the diagram shown below on the left, compares her work with Kenneth, who used equations, as shown on the right. Then Mr. Harris has the students repeat the process, finding another classmate and holding another share-and-compare session.

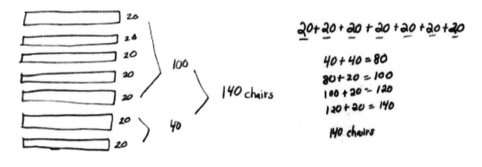

Jasmine's drawing   Kenneth's equations

Mr. Harris begins the whole-class discussion by summarizing the goal for the lesson as understanding how the different representations are related to the operation of multiplication. He first asks students to identify and explain how different visual representations show both the number of equal groups and the amount in each group as a structure of

Fig. 10. A third-grade lesson emphasizing mathematical representations to solve a task on setting up chairs for a band concert

multiplication. This prompts the students to compare diagrams with equal groups, arrays, and area models and discuss how they are similar and different. The students comment that it is easy to see the number of chairs in each row in some of the diagrams but not in others. Mr. Harris then writes 7 × 20 on the board and asks the students to explain how the expression matches each of the diagrams.

Finally, Mr. Harris has the students discuss and compare the representations of those students who considered the aisle and worked with tens rather than with twenties, such as Amanda, whose work is shown below. He asks them to take this final step, knowing that this informal experience and discussion of the distributive property will be important in subsequent lessons.

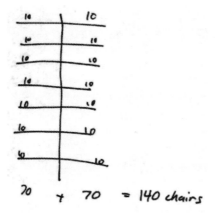

Amanda's work with tens

Fig. 10. *Continued*

Mr. Harris selects the task about the chairs for the band concert to focus on a problem situation that can be represented with arrays. The goal for the lesson is for students to understand how the structure of multiplication is evident within and among different representations. He chooses the numbers purposefully to build his students' conceptual understanding of multiplying one-digit whole numbers by multiples of 10, using strategies based on place value and properties of operations. He allows students to select and discuss their choices to represent the problem situation. Mr. Harris pays close attention to what students are doing, and the questions that he poses as they work and during the whole-class discussion help his students make explicit connections among the representations in ways that further their understanding of the central mathematical ideas of the lesson.

Teacher and student actions

Effective teaching emphasizes using and making connections among mathematical representations to deepen student understanding of concepts and procedures, support mathematical discourse among students, and serve as tools for solving problems. As students use and make connections among contextual, physical, visual, verbal, and symbolic representations, they grow in their appreciation of mathematics as a unified, coherent discipline. The teacher and student actions listed in the table below provide a summary of what teachers and students do in using mathematical representations in teaching and learning mathematics.

Use and connect mathematical representations Teacher and student actions	
What are *teachers* doing?	**What are *students* doing?**
Selecting tasks that allow students to decide which representations to use in making sense of the problems.	Using multiple forms of representations to make sense of and understand mathematics.
Allocating substantial instructional time for students to use, discuss, and make connections among representations.	Describing and justifying their mathematical understanding and reasoning with drawings, diagrams, and other representations.
Introducing forms of representations that can be useful to students.	Making choices about which forms of representations to use as tools for solving problems.
Asking students to make math drawings or use other visual supports to explain and justify their reasoning.	Sketching diagrams to make sense of problem situations.
Focusing students' attention on the structure or essential features of mathematical ideas that appear, regardless of the representation.	Contextualizing mathematical ideas by connecting them to real-world situations.
Designing ways to elicit and assess students' abilities to use representations meaningfully to solve problems.	Considering the advantages or suitability of using various representations when solving problems.

Facilitate Meaningful Mathematical Discourse

Effective teaching of mathematics facilitates discourse among students to build shared understanding of mathematical ideas by analyzing and comparing student approaches and arguments.

Effective mathematics teaching engages students in discourse to advance the mathematical learning of the whole class. Mathematical discourse includes the purposeful exchange of ideas through classroom discussion, as well as through other forms of verbal, visual, and written communication. The discourse in the mathematics classroom gives students opportunities to share ideas and clarify understandings, construct convincing arguments regarding why and how things work, develop a language for expressing mathematical ideas, and learn to see things from other perspectives (NCTM 1991, 2000).

Discussion

Discourse that focuses on tasks that promote reasoning and problem solving is a primary mechanism for developing conceptual understanding and meaningful learning of mathematics (Michaels, O'Connor, and Resnick 2008). According to Carpenter, Franke, and Levi (2003, p. 6),

> Students who learn to articulate and justify their own mathematical ideas, reason through their own and others' mathematical explanations, and provide a rationale for their answers develop a deep understanding that is critical to their future success in mathematics and related fields.

Although discourse provides important opportunities for students to learn what mathematics is *and* how one does it, creating a culture of discourse in the mathematics classroom also presents challenges. Teachers must determine how to build on and honor student thinking while ensuring that the mathematical ideas at the heart of the lesson remain prominent in class discussions (Engle and Conant 2002). For example, in orchestrating a class discussion of student approaches to solving a task, the teacher must decide what approaches to share, the order in which they should be shared, and the questions that will help students make connections among the different strategies and the key disciplinary ideas that are driving the lesson. Such discussions can easily become little more than elaborate show-and-tell sessions (Wood and Turner-Vorbeck 2001) in which it is not clear what each solution adds to students' developing understanding or how it advances the mathematical storyline of the lesson. Smith and Stein (2011) describe five practices for effectively using student responses in whole-class discussions:

1. *Anticipating* student responses prior to the lesson
2. *Monitoring* students' work on and engagement with the tasks
3. *Selecting* particular students to present their mathematical work
4. *Sequencing* students' responses in a specific order for discussion
5. *Connecting* different students' responses and connecting the responses to key mathematical ideas

Students must also have opportunities to talk with, respond to, and question one another as part of the discourse community, in ways that support the mathematics learning of all students in the class. Hufferd-Ackles, Fuson, and Sherin (2004) describe a framework for moving toward a classroom community centered on discourse. They examine how teachers and students proceed through levels in shifting from a classroom in which teachers play the leading role in pursuing student mathematical thinking to one in which they assist students in taking on important roles. The framework describes growth in five components (Hufferd-Ackles, Fuson, and Sherin 2004):

1. How the teacher supports student engagement

2. Who serves as the questioner and what kinds of questions are posed

3. Who provides what kinds of explanations

4. How mathematical representations are used

5. How much responsibility students share for the learning of their peers and themselves

Figure 11 shows a table developed by Hufford-Ackles, Fuson, and Sherin (2014) to describe the levels of classroom discourse through which teachers and their students advance.

Illustration

Mr. Donnelly and his seventh-grade students are studying proportional relationships and their use to solve real-world and mathematical problems. As part of this work, Mr. Donnelly wants his students to be able to identify multiplicative relationships between quantities and recognize three strategies for solving such problems—scaling up, scale factor, and unit rate. He has selected the Candy Jar task, shown in figure 12, for the lesson, since it is aligned with his goals, provides opportunities for high-level reasoning, and offers multiple entry points. Figure 13 shows Mr. Donnelly's lesson on the Candy Jar task.

Suppose you have a new candy jar with the same ratio of Jolly Ranchers (JR) to jawbreakers (JB) as shown in the picture, but it contains 100 Jolly Ranchers.

How many jawbreakers do you have?

Justify your answer.

Note: In the picture, Jolly Ranchers are represented by 5 rectangles, and jawbreakers are shown by 13 circles.

Fig. 12. The Candy Jar task. Adapted from Smith and colleagues (2005).

	Teacher role	Questioning	Explaining mathematical thinking	Mathematical representations	Building student responsibility within the community
Level 0	Teacher is at the front of the room and dominates conversation.	Teacher is only questioner. Questions serve to keep students listening to teacher. Students give short answers and respond to teacher only.	Teacher questions focus on correctness. Students provide short answer-focused responses. Teacher may give answers.	Representations are missing, or teacher shows them to students.	Culture supports students keeping ideas to themselves or just providing answers when asked.
Level 1	Teacher encourages the sharing of math ideas and directs speaker to talk to the class, not to the teacher only.	Teacher questions begin to focus on student thinking and less on answers. Only teacher asks questions.	Teacher probes student thinking somewhat. One or two strategies may be elicited. Teacher may fill in an explanation. Students provide brief descriptions of their thinking in response to teacher probing.	Students learn to create math drawings to depict their mathematical thinking.	Students believe that their ideas are accepted by the classroom community. They begin to listen to one another supportively and to re-state in their own words what another student has said.
Level 2	Teacher facilitates conversation between students, and encourages students to ask questions of one another.	Teacher asks probing questions and facilitates some student-to-student talk. Students ask questions of one another with prompting from teacher.	Teacher probes more deeply to learn about student thinking. Teacher elicits multiple strategies. Students respond to teacher probing and volunteer their thinking. Students begin to defend their answers.	Students label their math drawings so that others are able to follow their mathematical thinking.	Students believe that they are math learners and that their ideas and the ideas of their classmates are important. They listen actively so that they can contribute significantly.
Level 3	Students carry the conversation themselves. Teacher only guides from the periphery of the conversation. Teacher waits for students to clarify thinking of others.	Student-to-student talk is student initiated. Students ask questions and listen to responses. Many questions ask "why" and call for justification. Teacher questions may still guide discourse.	Teacher follows student explanations closely. Teacher asks students to contrast strategies. Students defend and justify their answers with little prompting from the teacher.	Students follow and help shape the descriptions of others' math thinking through math drawings and may suggest edits in others' math drawings.	Students believe that they are math leaders and can help shape the thinking of others. They help shape others' math thinking in supportive, collegial ways and accept the same support from others.

Fig. 11. Levels of classroom discourse. From Hufford-Ackles, Fuson, and Sherin (2014), table 1.

Mr. Donnelly monitors his students as they work in small groups on the Candy Jar task, providing support as needed and taking note of their strategies. He notices that students who use the scaling up strategy do so in different ways. Some use a table that shows a constant increase of 5 Jolly Ranchers and 13 jawbreakers (see solution 1 below), some use a ratio table that contains different multiples of 5 and 13, and some even draw pictures of candy jars. He decides to have the groups who created solutions 1, 2, and 3, shown below, present their work (in this order), since these groups used the strategies that he is targeting (i.e., scaling up, scale factor, and unit rate). This sequencing reflects the sophistication and frequency of strategies (i.e., most groups used a version of the scaling up strategy, and only one group used the unit rate strategy).

Solution 1. Scaling up reasoning

Student explanation: "I started with 5 Jolly Ranchers (JR) and 13 jawbreakers (JB), and I just kept adding on 5 JR and 13 JB every time until I got to 100 JR. Then I saw that I had 260 JB."

JR	5	10	15	20	25	30	35	40	45	50	55	60	65	70	75	80	85	90	95	100
JB	13	26	39	52	65	78	91	104	117	130	143	156	169	182	195	208	221	234	247	260

Solution 2. Scale factor reasoning

Student explanation: "You had to multiply the five Jolly Ranchers by 20 to get 100, so you'd also have to multiply the 13 jawbreakers by 20, getting 260."

$$(\times 20)$$
$$5 \text{ JR} \longrightarrow 100 \text{ JR}$$
$$13 \text{ JB} \longrightarrow 260 \text{ JB}$$
$$(\times 20)$$

Solution 3. Unit rate reasoning

Student explanation: "Since the ratio is 5 Jolly Ranchers (JR) for 13 jawbreakers (JB), you could give each JR that you have 2 JB. That would use up 10 of them, and then you still have 3 JB that have to be shared. So to distribute the 3 JB to the 5 JR, that would be $3 \div 5 = 0.6$ of a JB, so putting that together would give the ratio of 1 JR to 2.6 JB. So then you just multiply 100 by 2.6."

$$(\times 100)$$
$$1 \text{ JR} \longrightarrow 100 \text{ JR}$$
$$2.6 \text{ JB} \longrightarrow 260 \text{ JB}$$
$$(\times 100)$$

During the discussion, Mr. Donnelly asks the presenters to explain what they did and why, and he invites other students to consider whether the approach makes sense and to ask questions. He makes a point of labeling each of the three strategies, asking students which one is most efficient in solving this particular task, and he poses questions that help students make connections among the strategies and with the key ideas that he is targeting.

Fig. 13. Mr. Donnelly's implementation of the Candy Jar task.
Solutions adapted from Smith and colleagues (2005).

Specifically, he wants students to see that the scale factor is the same as the number of entries in the table used for scaling up. In other words, it would take 20 candy jars with the same number of Jolly Ranchers and jawbreakers as the original jar to make the new candy jar. Mr. Donnelly then will have his students compare this result with the unit rate, which is the factor that relates the number of Jolly Ranchers and the number of jawbreakers in each column of the table in solution 1 (e.g., $5 \times 2.6 = 13$, just as $55 \times 2.6 = 143$, just as $100 \times 2.6 = 260$).

Toward the end of the lesson, Mr. Donnelly places the solution shown below as solution 4 on the document camera in the classroom and asks students to decide whether or not this is a viable approach to solving the task and to justify their answers.

Solution 4. Incorrect additive reasoning

Student explanation: "100 Jolly Ranchers is 95 more than the 5 I started with. So I will need 95 more jawbreakers than the 13 I started with."

$$5 \text{ JR} + 95 \text{ JR} = 100 \text{ JR}$$

$$13 \text{ JB} + 95 \text{ JB} = 108 \text{ JB}$$

Mr. Donnelly gives the students five minutes to write a response, and he collects their responses as they leave the room to go to the next class. He expects their responses to give him some insight into whether they are coming to understand that for ratios to remain constant, their numerators and denominators must grow at a rate that is multiplicative, not additive.

Fig. 13. *Continued*

Mr. Donnelly keeps close track of what his students are doing as they explore the task (*monitoring*) so that he is positioned to make strategic choices regarding which solutions to highlight during the whole-class discussion (*selecting*) and in what order (*sequencing*). He selects three groups to present their work—each of which used one of the strategies that he has targeted in his goal for the lesson. By making deliberate choices about what to focus on during the whole-class discussion, he is able to use the discussion time to engage students productively in a thoughtful consideration of a small number of approaches and the connections among them (*connecting*). His decision to end the class by asking students to write individual critiques of a response that uses incorrect additive reasoning gives him a way of assessing the extent to which his students understand that the relationship between the types of candies is multiplicative, not additive.

Mr. Donnelly facilitates rather than directs the discussion. By building on the work produced by students, he positions them as "authors" of the mathematics and engages them in rich discourse about an important set of ideas related to ratios and proportional relationships. Although he asks questions and provides information (e.g., labels for the strategies) to ensure that the mathematics learning goals are met, he does so in a way that gives the students ownership of their learning. Mr. Donnelly is clearly in charge of the lesson, but he offers guidance mostly under the radar, so that it does not impinge on students' growing mathematical authority.

Teacher and student actions

Mathematical discourse among students is central to meaningful learning of mathematics. Teachers carefully prepare and purposefully facilitate discourse, such as whole-class discussions that build on student thinking and guide the learning of the class in a productive disciplinary direction. Students are active members of the discourse community as they explain their reasoning and consider the mathematical explanations and strategies of their classmates. The actions listed in the table below provide some guidance on what teachers and students do as they engage in meaningful discourse in the mathematics classroom.

Facilitate meaningful mathematical discourse Teacher and student actions	
What are *teachers* doing?	**What are *students* doing?**
Engaging students in purposeful sharing of mathematical ideas, reasoning, and approaches, using varied representations.	Presenting and explaining ideas, reasoning, and representations to one another in pair, small-group, and whole-class discourse.
Selecting and sequencing student approaches and solution strategies for whole-class analysis and discussion.	Listening carefully to and critiquing the reasoning of peers, using examples to support or counterexamples to refute arguments.
Facilitating discourse among students by positioning them as authors of ideas, who explain and defend their approaches.	Seeking to understand the approaches used by peers by asking clarifying questions, trying out others' strategies, and describing the approaches used by others.
Ensuring progress toward mathematical goals by making explicit connections to student approaches and reasoning.	Identifying how different approaches to solving a task are the same and how they are different.

Pose Purposeful Questions

Effective teaching of mathematics uses purposeful questions to assess and advance students' reasoning and sense making about important mathematical ideas and relationships.

Effective mathematics teaching relies on questions that encourage students to explain and reflect on their thinking as an essential component of meaningful mathematical discourse. Purposeful questions allow teachers to discern what students know and adapt lessons to meet varied levels of understanding, help students make important mathematical connections, and support students in posing their own questions. However, merely asking questions is not enough to ensure that students make sense of mathematics and advance their reasoning. Two critical issues must be considered—the types of questions that teachers ask and the pattern of questioning that they use.

Discussion

Researchers have created a variety of frameworks to categorize the types of questions that teachers ask (e.g., Boaler and Brodie 2004; Chapin and O'Connor 2007). Though the categories differ across frameworks, commonalities exist among the types of questions. For example, the frameworks generally include questions that ask students to recall information, as well as questions that ask students to explain their reasoning. Figure 14 displays a set of question types that synthesizes key aspects of these frameworks that are particularly important for mathematics teaching. Although the question types differ with respect to the level of thinking required in a response, all of the question types are necessary in the interactions among teachers and students. For example, questions that gather information are needed to establish what students know, while questions that encourage reflection and justification are essential to reveal student reasoning.

Question type		Description	Examples
1	Gathering information	Students recall facts, definitions, or procedures.	When you write an equation, what does the equal sign tell you?
			What is the formula for finding the area of a rectangle?
			What does the interquartile range indicate for a set of data?
2	Probing thinking	Students explain, elaborate, or clarify their thinking, including articulating the steps in solution methods or the completion of a task.	As you drew that number line, what decisions did you make so that you could represent 7 fourths on it?
			Can you show and explain more about how you used a table to find the answer to the Smartphone Plans task?
			It is still not clear how you figured out that 20 was the scale factor, so can you explain it another way?

Fig. 14. A framework for types of questions used in mathematics teaching

Question type		Description	Examples
3	Making the mathematics visible	Students discuss mathematical structures and make connections among mathematical ideas and relationships.	What does your equation have to do with the band concert situation? How does that array relate to multiplication and division? In what ways might the normal distribution apply to this situation?
4	Encouraging reflection and justification	Students reveal deeper understanding of their reasoning and actions, including making an argument for the validity of their work.	How might you prove that 51 is the solution? How do you know that the sum of two odd numbers will always be even? Why does plan A in the Smartphone Plans task start out cheaper but become more expensive in the long run?

Fig. 14. *Continued*

While the *types* of questions that teachers ask are important, so are the *patterns* of questions that they use during teacher-student interactions (Walsh and Sattes 2005). In the Initiate-Response-Evaluate (I-R-E) pattern, the teacher starts by asking a question to gather information, generally with a specific response in mind; a student responds; and then the teacher evaluates the response (Mehan 1979). It is not uncommon for teachers to allocate less than five seconds for a student to respond, and to take even less time to consider the answer themselves. This pattern of questioning generally affords very limited opportunities for students to think and provides teachers with no access to whether or how students are making sense of mathematics. Other questioning patterns involve more than asking recall questions. Two of these patterns of questioning are *funneling* and *focusing* (Herbel-Eisenmann and Breyfogle 2005; Wood 1998).

The funneling pattern of questioning involves using a set of questions to lead students to a desired procedure or conclusion, while giving limited attention to student responses that veer from the desired path. The teacher has decided on a particular path for the discussion to follow and leads the students along that path, not allowing students to make their own connections or build their own understanding of the targeted mathematical concepts. The I-R-E pattern is closely akin to funneling, though higher-level questions may be part of the funneling pattern.

In contrast, a focusing pattern of questioning involves the teacher in attending to what the students are thinking, pressing them to communicate their thoughts clearly, and expecting them to reflect on their thoughts and those of their classmates. The teacher who uses this pattern of questioning is open to a task being investigated in multiple ways. On the basis of content knowledge related to the topic and knowledge of student learning, the teacher plans questions and outlines key points that should become salient in the lesson.

Illustration

Figure 15 shows two high school teachers' implementation of the Coin Circulation task in their classrooms. They choose the task because it provides an opportunity for students to summarize, represent, and interpret data and to further understand and evaluate random processes underlying statistical investigations. In particular, students represent data with plots on the real number line and interpret differences in shape, center, and spread in the context of the data set.

Students in two high school classrooms are investigating how much money it costs to mint coins. As part of the investigation, the students decide that it would be helpful to determine the approximate number of years that a coin stays in circulation. Rather than studying all different types of coins, the students choose to collect data about the ages of pennies. This sets the stage for the students to investigate the question, "How many years does a penny stay in circulation?"

The teachers' mathematics learning goals for the task are for students to collect data, analyze the data, and reach a conclusion, as well as to identify the limitations of this investigation with respect to its sampling method. Specifically, the teachers want the students to recognize that the results do not generalize to a larger population.

Both teachers ask all the students to bring in pennies. The goal for each class is to bring in the equivalent of about one roll for every two or three students. Small groups sort their pennies by the year of minting and determine the age of each coin. The data from the entire class is recorded in a table on the board. The small groups then create dot plots and box plots similar to those shown below, based on the age of the coins.

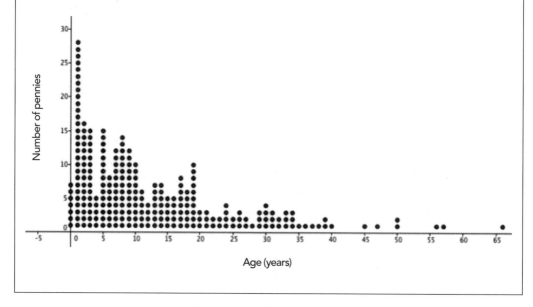

Fig. 15. The Coin Circulation task

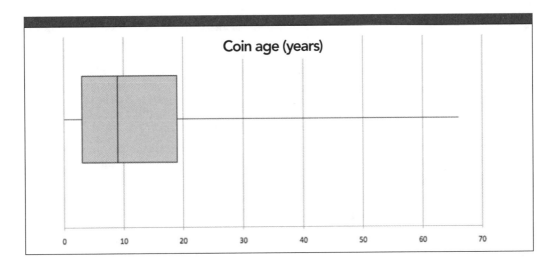

Fig. 15. *Continued*

Although the task engages the students in both classrooms in reasoning and problem solving, the teachers use different questioning patterns. The excerpts from the whole-class discussions shown in figure 16 illustrate the two teachers' questioning patterns.

Questioning pattern: Funneling	Questioning pattern: Focusing
T: What do you notice about the graph? [*waits briefly*] Do you see a pattern in the data? [*waits briefly again*] What are the measures of center for the pennies?	T: What things do you notice or wonder about the age of pennies?
S1: The mean is about 12.9 years, and the median is about 9 years.	S1: It doesn't seem like many of them are very old.
T: What does the box plot tell us about the variability of the data?	T: What about the graph makes you say that?
S2: It has a long tail on one side.	S1: There's a big mound for newer pennies.
T: That may be true, but what about the interquartile range—the IQR? What does it tell us?	T: Is there anything else that you notice?
S3: Where most of the pennies occur.	S2: I found the interquartile range and saw that most pennies are from 3 to 19 years old.
T: Is that really what the IQR tells us? What does each part of the box plot stand for?	T: Explain to us what the interquartile range tells us.
	S2: It is where most of the pennies occur.
	T: What do you mean by "most of the pennies"?

Fig. 16. A comparison of questioning patterns on the Coin Circulation task in two classrooms. (*T* is *Teacher*, *S1* is *Student 1*, and so on.)

Questioning pattern: Funneling	Questioning pattern: Focusing
S4: Each part is 25 percent.	S2: Well, I mean the middle 50 percent. I thought the graph made it hard to tell where things really were. It doesn't look normal, so I couldn't use the middle 68 percent thing we talked about.
T: Yes, so what else?	
S5: The middle is 50 percent of the pennies and is from 3 to 19 years old.	
T: Good. What can we say about pennies on the basis of this information?	T: I'm not sure I understand. Can someone else comment on what she's saying?
S6: That most of them are about 10 years old.	S3: She means that since there's a tail, the graph isn't like the normal curves we studied. If it were, we could approximate where the most likely ages are—like 68 percent of the data would be within one standard deviation of the mean.
T: But since these are pennies, what does that tell us about all coins?	
S7: That coins will be about 10 years old.	
T: Well, 10 years is for pennies, but this wouldn't necessarily be the same for, say, quarters. Why not?	[More discussion follows, and the students determine that 75 percent of the pennies are not more than 19 years old.]
	T: Would I be correct if I said that a fifty-cent piece would probably be no more than 19 years old?
	S4: Yes, because these coins were a random sample, and that means we can generalize.
	S5: But we looked at pennies, so we can't generalize to quarters. People use pennies more.
	T: What do you mean by that?
	S5: Pennies may wear out. We don't know about other coins from our sample, because quarters would be a different population.

Fig. 16. *Continued*

In the funneling example, the teacher wants students to look at the measures of center and the dispersion of the data. The dialogue demonstrates a reliance on gathering-of-information questions. Some recall of information is necessary so that the teacher knows the baseline of the students' thinking. But questions that probe for understanding need to be part of a questioning pattern that advances student reasoning. As this funneling dialogue moves forward, the teacher has the students look at the center and spread of the data to draw a conclusion and finally asks a higher-level question: "What can we say about pennies on the basis of this information?" Because the students have not been given an opportunity to think deeply enough about what the data tells them about the circulation of pennies, they can give only superficial responses to this question. This example illustrates a far-too-common pattern of questioning, in which the teacher initially uses a probing question but allows little wait time and immediately follows up with questions that become more directed toward one particular answer.

By contrast, the focusing example illustrates how the teacher purposefully blends all four types of questions. Some questions have been planned in advance of the lesson, along with consideration of possible student responses. Other questions are formulated on the spot, in response to student statements and actions during the lesson. Throughout the dialogue, the teacher strives to include questions that push students to clarify their ideas and make the mathematics visible, with the aim of deepening students' mathematical understanding in alignment with the intended learning goals.

Teacher and student actions

In effective teaching, teachers use a variety of question types to assess and gather evidence of student thinking, including questions that gather information, probe understanding, make the mathematics visible, and ask students to reflect on and justify their reasoning. Teachers then use patterns of questioning that focus on and extend students' current ideas to advance student understanding and sense making about important mathematical ideas and relationships. The teacher and student actions listed in the table below provide a summary of using questions purposefully in the mathematics classroom.

Pose purposeful questions Teacher and student actions	
What are _teachers_ doing?	**What are _students_ doing?**
Advancing student understanding by asking questions that build on, but do not take over or funnel, student thinking. Making certain to ask questions that go beyond gathering information to probing thinking and requiring explanation and justification. Asking intentional questions that make the mathematics more visible and accessible for student examination and discussion. Allowing sufficient wait time so that more students can formulate and offer responses.	Expecting to be asked to explain, clarify, and elaborate on their thinking. Thinking carefully about how to present their responses to questions clearly, without rushing to respond quickly. Reflecting on and justifying their reasoning, not simply providing answers. Listening to, commenting on, and questioning the contributions of their classmates.

Build Procedural Fluency
from Conceptual Understanding

Effective teaching of mathematics builds fluency with procedures on a foundation of conceptual understanding so that students, over time, become skillful in using procedures flexibly as they solve contextual and mathematical problems.

Effective mathematics teaching focuses on the development of *both* conceptual understanding *and* procedural fluency. Major reports have identified the importance of an integrated and balanced development of concepts and procedures in learning mathematics (National Mathematics Advisory Panel 2008; National Research Council 2001). Furthermore, NCTM (1989, 2000) and CCSSM (NGA Center and CCSSO 2010) emphasize that procedural fluency follows and builds on a foundation of conceptual understanding, strategic reasoning, and problem solving.

Discussion

When procedures are connected with the underlying concepts, students have better retention of the procedures and are more able to apply them in new situations (Fuson, Kalchman, and Bransford 2005). Martin (2009, p. 165) describes some of the reasons that fluency depends on and extends from conceptual understanding:

> To use mathematics effectively, students must be able to do much more than carry out mathematical procedures. They must know which procedure is appropriate and most productive in a given situation, what a procedure accomplishes, and what kind of results to expect. Mechanical execution of procedures without understanding their mathematical basis often leads to bizarre results.

Fluency is not a simple idea. Being fluent means that students are able to choose flexibly among methods and strategies to solve contextual and mathematical problems, they understand and are able to explain their approaches, and they are able to produce accurate answers efficiently. Fluency builds from initial exploration and discussion of number concepts to using informal reasoning strategies based on meanings and properties of the operations to the eventual use of general methods as tools in solving problems. This sequence is beneficial whether students are building toward fluency with single- and multi-digit computation with whole numbers or fluency with, for example, fraction operations, proportional relationships, measurement formulas, or algebraic procedures.

Computational fluency is strongly related to number sense and involves so much more than the conventional view of it encompasses. Developing students' computational fluency extends far beyond having students memorize facts or a series of steps unconnected to understanding (Baroody 2006; Griffin 2005). A rush to fluency, however, undermines students' confidence and interest in mathematics and is considered a cause of mathematics anxiety (Ashcraft 2002; Ramirez et al. 2013). Further, early work with reasoning strategies is related to algebraic reasoning. As students learn how quantities can be taken apart and put back together in different ways (i.e., decomposition and composition of numbers), they establish a basis for understanding properties of the operations. Students need this early foundation for meaningful learning of more formal algebraic concepts and procedures throughout elementary school and into middle and high school (Carpenter, Franke, and Levi 2003; Griffin 2003; Common Core State Standards Writing Team 2011).

In meaningful learning of basic number combinations (i.e., addition and subtraction within 20 and multiplication and division within 100), students progress through well-documented phases toward fluency (Baroody 2006; Baroody, Bajwa, and Eiland 2009; Carpenter et al. 1999). Students begin by using objects, visual representations, and verbal counting, and then they progress to reasoning strategies using number relationships and properties. For example, to solve $8 + 4$, a first grader might count on from 8 early in the school year, whereas later in the year the same student might reason that since $8 + 2$ is 10, then $8 + 4$ must be 2 more than 10, or 12. A third grader might initially use repeated addition to solve 4×6 and then progress to reason that 2 sixes are 12, so 4 sixes must be double that amount, which is 24. This approach supports students, over time, in knowing, understanding, and being able to use their knowledge of number combinations meaningfully in new situations.

Learning procedures for multi-digit computation needs to build from an understanding of their mathematical basis (Fuson and Beckmann 2012/2013; Russell 2000). For example, consider the work in figure 17 by David and Anna, two fourth graders, on a multiplication problem, $57 \times 4 = \square$, and their explanations of what they have done.

David's solution	Anna's solution
$$\begin{array}{r} {}^{+2} \\ 57 \\ \times\ \ 4 \\ \hline 288 \end{array}$$	4×57 $4 \times 50 = 200$ $4 \times 7 = 28$ $200 + 28 = 228$
I multiplied 7 and 4 and got 28. I put down the 8 and carried the 2. Then I added the 2 and the 5 and got 7 and multiplied it by 4 and got 28. I put down the 28 and got 288.	I did it in parts. First I multiplied 4 x 50 and got 200. Then I multiplied 4 and 7 and got 28. Then I just added those two parts together to get the answer.

Fig. 17. David's and Anna's solutions to a multiplication problem.
Adapted from Russell (2000).

David's faulty application of the multiplication algorithm leads to an incorrect answer that he should have recognized as too large (i.e., a reasonable answer must be less than 4×60). Anna's solution, by contrast, shows her understanding that 57 can be partitioned into tens and ones, that each quantity can be multiplied by 4 (an application of the distributive property), and that those new quantities can then be combined.

Similarly, a high school student who does not understand the distance formula,

$$d = \sqrt{(x_1 - x_2)^2 + (y_1 - y_2)^2},$$

may have trouble accurately recalling it and applying it appropriately to problem situations. By contrast, a student who understands that the formula is an application of the Pythagorean theorem (i.e., the distance between two points can be thought of as the hypotenuse of a right triangle) can use an understanding of this underlying relationship to solve a problem involving the distance between two points correctly (Martin 2009).

Clearly, students need procedures that they can use with understanding on a broad class of problems. This raises questions regarding *how* students can move most effectively toward fluency with general methods or algorithms, as well as what defines an algorithm. Fuson and Beckmann (2012/2013) argue that a standard algorithm is defined by its mathematical approach and not by the way in which the steps in the approach are recorded. They suggest that variations in written notation are not only acceptable but indeed valuable in supporting students' understanding of the base-ten system and properties of the operations. They also emphasize the importance of understanding, explaining, and visualizing: "Standard algorithms are to be understood and explained and related to visual models before there is any focus on fluency" (p. 28).

For example, as figure 18 illustrates, the conventional algorithm for multi-digit multiplication is difficult to understand, whereas the three alternative methods shown are more transparent with respect to the central mathematical features of place-value meanings and properties of the operations (Fuson 2003). The diagrams show the multiplication of tens and ones and the relative size (in area) of the partial products. The accessible algorithm shows a clear record of the four pairs of numbers that are multiplied. This progression also supports students in establishing a basis from which to apply and extend these understandings to operations with rational numbers and algebraic expressions.

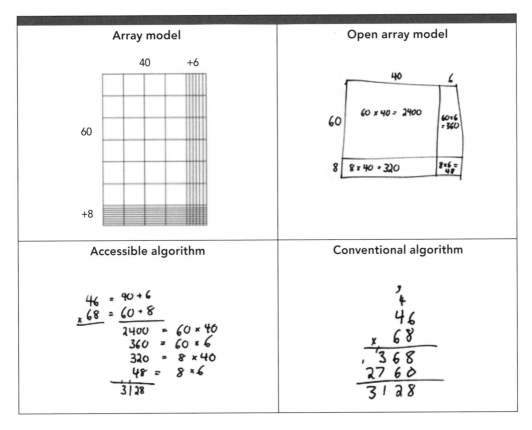

Fig. 18. Methods for multi-digit multiplication, using 68 × 46.
Adapted from Fuson (2003, p. 303).

In moving to fluency, students also need opportunities to rehearse or practice strategies and procedures to solidify their knowledge. However, giving students too many practice problems too soon is an ineffective approach to fluency. Students need opportunities to practice on a moderate number of carefully selected problems after they have established a strong conceptual foundation and the ability to explain the mathematical basis for a strategy or procedure. At that point, providing students with practice on a small number of problems, "spacing" or distributing these over time, and including feedback on student performance support learning outcomes (Pashler et al. 2007; Rohrer 2009; Rohrer and Taylor 2007).

Similarly, practice with basic number combinations should occur after students can explain and justify their use of efficient reasoning strategies. A word of caution is important in regard to timed tests. The premature and overuse of such tests may hinder students' mathematical proficiency and lower their confidence in themselves as learners of mathematics (Boaler 2012; Seeley 2009). Practice with basic number combinations should focus on solidifying students' use of an efficient strategy for specific number combinations (Rathmell 2005; Thornton 1978). Isaacs and Carroll (1999) suggest that practice be brief, engaging, purposeful, and distributed. For example, practice can target specific strategies, such as making a ten for addition or doubling a known fact for multiplication, and can be embedded in problem-solving tasks and games (Crespo, Kyriakides, and McGee 2005).

Illustration

Mr. Donnelly's use of the lesson featuring the Candy Jar task, illustrated in figure 13, is an important step in building his students' fluency in solving problems that involve proportional relationships. Mr. Donnelly helps his students understand that the ratios need to remain constant and that they can use different approaches to preserve this constant multiplicative relationship between the numerator and the denominator. Over time, Mr. Donnelly will need to discuss the efficiency of some strategies over others (e.g., using the scale factor is usually more efficient than scaling up by using a table), and he will need to provide examples of problems that specific strategies would be particularly useful in solving. Ultimately, Mr. Donnelly will want to give his students problems in which neither the unit rate nor the scale factor are integers (e.g., $5/13 = 127/x$) and ask students to devise methods for finding the missing value. Students might generate either of the approaches shown in figure 19, the scale factor method and the unit rate method.

Consider the reasoning that underlies each of these methods and how each is clearly grounded in an understanding of ratio concepts and multiplicative relationships. Mr. Donnelly could then ask his students to consider the generalizability of these approaches as another step toward fluency in solving problems involving proportional relationships.

Teacher and student actions

Effective teaching not only acknowledges the importance of both conceptual understanding and procedural fluency but also ensures that the learning of procedures is developed over time, on a strong foundation of understanding and the use of student-generated strategies in solving problems. This approach supports students in developing the ability to understand and explain their use of procedures, choose flexibly among methods and strategies to solve contextual and mathematical problems, and produce accurate answers efficiently. The actions identified in the table at the right summarize what teachers and students are doing in mathematics classrooms to build procedural fluency from conceptual understanding and problem-solving experiences.

$$\frac{5}{13} = \frac{127}{x}$$

Scale factor method	Unit rate method

JR: $5n = 127$

$n = 25.4$ ← scale factor

JB: $13 \cdot 25.4 = 330.2$

$5n = 13$

Unit rate $= 2.6$

So $1 \, JR = 2.6 \, JB$

$127 \cdot 2.6 = 330.2$ jaw breakers in the new jar

Student explanation: "The original jar contained 5 Jolly Ranchers, but the new jar contains 127 Jolly Ranchers, so 5 times some number is 127. So, 127 ÷ 5 = 25.4. So, this is the factor that I need to use because the new jar has to have 25.4 times more Jolly Ranchers. Since the original jar had 13 jawbreakers and I need to keep the same ratio, I needed to multiply 13 by the same scale factor, so 13 × 25.4 = 330.2 jawbreakers in the new jar."

Student explanation: "The ratio is 5 Jolly Ranchers for every 13 jawbreakers, so 5 times some number is 13. If I distribute the 13 jawbreakers equally among the 5 Jolly Ranchers, 13 ÷ 5 = 2.6, which gives the ratio of 1 Jolly Rancher for every 2.6 jawbreakers, so 2.6 is the unit rate. Since I have 127 Jolly Ranchers, or units, in the new jar, I have to multiply this by the unit rate, so 127 × 2.6 = 330.2 jawbreakers.

"Well, 330.2 is the exact answer. But since jawbreakers have to be whole numbers, the answer to problem is 330 jawbreakers."

Fig. 19. Student approaches to the Candy Jar task, leading to general methods

Build procedural fluency from conceptual understanding Teacher and student actions	
What are *teachers* doing?	**What are *students* doing?**
Providing students with opportunities to use their own reasoning strategies and methods for solving problems. Asking students to discuss and explain why the procedures that they are using work to solve particular problems. Connecting student-generated strategies and methods to more efficient procedures as appropriate.	Making sure that they understand and can explain the mathematical basis for the procedures that they are using. Demonstrating flexible use of strategies and methods while reflecting on which procedures seem to work best for specific types of problems. Determining whether specific approaches generalize to a broad class of problems.

Build procedural fluency from conceptual understanding Teacher and student actions, *continued*	
What are *teachers* doing?	What are *students* doing?
Using visual models to support students' understanding of general methods. Providing students with opportunities for distributed practice of procedures.	Striving to use procedures appropriately and efficiently.

Support Productive Struggle in Learning Mathematics

Effective teaching of mathematics consistently provides students, individually and collectively, with opportunities and supports to engage in productive struggle as they grapple with mathematical ideas and relationships.

Effective mathematics teaching supports students in struggling productively as they learn mathematics. Such instruction embraces a view of students' struggles as opportunities for delving more deeply into understanding the mathematical structure of problems and relationships among mathematical ideas, instead of simply seeking correct solutions. In contrast to productive struggle, unproductive struggle occurs when students "make no progress towards sense-making, explaining, or proceeding with a problem or task at hand" (Warshauer 2011, p. 21). A focus on student struggle is a necessary component of teaching that supports students' learning of mathematics with understanding (Hiebert and Grouws 2007). Teaching that embraces and uses productive struggle leads to long-term benefits, with students more able to apply their learning to new problem situations (Kapur 2010).

Discussion

In comparisons of mathematics teaching in the United States and in high-achieving countries, U.S. mathematics instruction has been characterized as rarely asking students to think and reason with or about mathematical ideas (Banilower et al. 2006; Hiebert and Stigler 2004). Teachers sometimes perceive student frustration or lack of immediate success as indicators that they have somehow failed their students. As a result, they jump in to "rescue" students by breaking down the task and guiding students step by step through the difficulties. Although well intentioned, such "rescuing" undermines the efforts of students, lowers the cognitive demand of the task, and deprives students of opportunities to engage fully in making sense of the mathematics (Reinhart 2000; Stein et al. 2009). As teachers plan lessons, key components for them to consider are the student struggles and misconceptions that might arise. Thinking about these in advance allows teachers to plan ways to support students productively without removing the opportunities for students to develop deeper understanding of the mathematics.

Mathematics classrooms that embrace productive struggle necessitate rethinking on the part of both students and teachers. Students must rethink what it means to be a successful learner of mathematics, and teachers must rethink what it means to be an effective teacher of mathematics. Figure 20 summarizes one such effort to redefine success in the mathematics classroom (Smith 2000), including expectations for students in regard to what it means to know and do mathematics, and actions for teachers with respect to what they can do to support students' learning, including acknowledging and using struggles as opportunities to learn.

Expectations for students	Teacher actions to support students	Classroom-based indicators of success
Most tasks that promote reasoning and problem solving take time to solve, and frustration may occur, but perseverance in the face of initial difficulty is important.	Use tasks that promote reasoning and problem solving; explicitly encourage students to persevere; find ways to support students without removing all the challenges in a task.	Students are engaged in the tasks and do not give up. The teacher supports students when they are "stuck" but does so in a way that keeps the thinking and reasoning at a high level.
Correct solutions are important, but so is being able to explain and discuss how one thought about and solved particular tasks.	Ask students to explain and justify how they solved a task. Value the quality of the explanation as much as the final solution.	Students explain how they solved a task and provide mathematical justifications for their reasoning.
Everyone has a responsibility and an obligation to make sense of mathematics by asking questions of peers and the teacher when he or she does not understand.	Give students the opportunity to discuss and determine the validity and appropriateness of strategies and solutions.	Students question and critique the reasoning of their peers and reflect on their own understanding.
Diagrams, sketches, and hands-on materials are important tools to use in making sense of tasks.	Give students access to tools that will support their thinking processes.	Students are able to use tools to solve tasks that they cannot solve without them.
Communicating about one's thinking during a task makes it possible for others to help that person make progress on the task.	Ask students to explain their thinking and pose questions that are based on students' reasoning, rather than on the way that the teacher is thinking about the task.	Students explain their thinking about a task to their peers and the teacher. The teacher asks probing questions based on the students' thinking.

Fig. 20. Redefining student and teacher success. Adapted from Smith (2000, p. 382).

Teachers greatly influence how students perceive and approach struggle in the mathematics classroom. Even young students can learn to value struggle as an expected and natural part of learning, as demonstrated by the class motto of one first-grade math class: "If you are not struggling, you are not learning" (Carter 2008, p. 136). Teachers must accept that struggle is important to students' learning of mathematics, convey this message to students, and provide time for them to try to work through their uncertainties. Unfortunately, this may not be enough, since some students will still simply shut down in the face of frustration, proclaim "I don't know," and give up. Dweck (2006) has shown that students with a fixed mindset—that is, those who believe that intelligence (especially math ability) is an innate trait—are more likely to give up when they encounter difficulties because they believe that learning mathematics should come naturally. By contrast, students with a growth mindset—that is, those who believe that intelligence can be developed through effort—are likely to persevere through a struggle because they see challenging work as an opportunity to learn and grow.

The fixed mindset appears to be more prevalent in mathematics than in other subject areas (Dweck 2008). Mindsets, however, can be changed when students realize that they are in control of how they approach and view their own abilities to learn (Blackwell, Trzesniewski, and Dweck 2007). It is important to note that even students who have always gotten good grades may have a fixed mindset. These higher-achieving students are often concerned about how smart they appear to be, so they prefer tasks that they can already do well and try to avoid tasks in which they may make mistakes. Dweck (2008, p. 8) offers important words of caution:

> For the last few decades many parents and educators have been more interested in making students feel good about themselves in math and science than in helping them achieve. Sometimes this may take the form of praising their intelligence or talent and sometimes this may take the form of relieving them of the responsibility of doing well, for example, by telling them they are not a "math person." Both of these strategies can promote a fixed mindset.

A key message from this research is that teachers must acknowledge and value students for their perseverance and effort in reasoning and sense making in mathematics and must provide students with specific descriptive feedback on their progress related to these efforts (Clarke 2003; Hattie and Timperley 2007). This behavior by teachers may include giving feedback to students that values their efforts at trying varied strategies in solving problems, their willingness to ask questions about specific aspects of the task, or their attempts to be precise in explanations and use of mathematical language. For example, if students need to be more precise in their written or verbal explanations, the teacher could provide feedback that details how their explanations either are, or are not, precise. The result will be the development of students who are more likely to embrace difficulties and uncertainties as natural opportunities in solving problems and maintain engagement and persistence in their mathematics learning. (For an example of a warm-up routine that engages students in an eighth-grade classroom in productive struggle, view "My Favorite No: Learning from Mistakes" [https://www.teachingchannel.org/videos/class-warm-up-routine].)

Illustration

Figure 21 illustrates how two teachers, Ms. Flahive and Ms. Ramirez, present a real-world task related to fractions to two classes of fifth-grade students. In both classrooms, some students are immediately at a loss, upset, and vocal about their feeling that they don't know what to do. The two teachers respond to their students' discomfort in different ways.

Ms. Flahive and Ms. Ramirez teach fifth grade and plan their lessons collaboratively. Their current instructional unit focuses on fractions. They have selected the Shopping Trip task shown below because they think it will be accessible to their students yet provoke some struggle and challenge, since a solution pathway is not straightforward. The mathematics goal for students is to draw on and apply their understanding of how to build non-unit fractions from unit fractions and to use visual representations to solve a multi-step word problem:

Shopping Trip Task

Joseph went to the mall with his friends to spend the money that he had received for his birthday. When he got home, he had $24 remaining. He had spent 3/5 of his birthday money at the mall on video games and food. How much money did he spend? How much money had he received for his birthday?

When Ms. Flahive and Ms. Ramirez present the problem in their classrooms, both teachers see students struggling to get started. Some students in both classrooms immediately raise their hands, saying, "I don't get it," or "I don't know what to do."

Ms. Flahive is very directive in her response to her students. She tells them to draw a rectangle and shows them how to divide it into fifths to represent what Joseph had spent and what he had left. She then guides her students step by step until they have labeled each one-fifth of the rectangle as worth $12, as shown below. Finally, she tells the students to use the information in the diagram to figure out the answers to the questions.

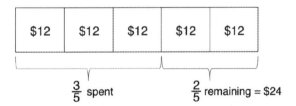

Ms. Ramirez approaches her students' struggles very differently. After she sees them struggling, she has them stop working on the problem and asks all the students to write down two things that they know about the problem and one thing that they wish they knew because it would help them make progress in solving the problem. Then Ms. Ramirez initiates a short class discussion in which several ideas are offered for what to do next. Suggestions include drawing a tape diagram or number line showing fifths, or just picking a number, such as $50 and proceeding through trial and error. Ms. Ramirez encourages the students to consider the various ideas that have been shared as they continue working on the task.

Fig. 21. Two teachers' responses to students' struggles to solve a multi-step word problem involving fractions

Ms. Flahive wants the students to be successful in figuring out the answer, so she begins to direct their work. Ms. Ramirez resists the temptation to step in but instead supports the students in considering what they know and what they need to figure out. As a result of these different approaches by the teachers to supporting struggling students, the students have very different opportunities to learn. Ms. Flahive's students learn that if you struggle and are vocal about your confusion, the teacher will ultimately tell you what to do; Ms. Ramirez's students learn that if you struggle and are at an impasse, the teacher will provide some assistance—but in the end you have to figure things out for yourself.

Teacher and student actions

Effective mathematics teaching uses students' struggles as valuable opportunities to deepen their understanding of mathematics. Students come to realize that they are capable of doing well in mathematics with effort and perseverance in reasoning, sense making, and problem solving. Teachers provide supports for students, individually and collectively, to work through uncertainties as they grapple with representing a mathematical relationship, explaining and justifying their reasoning, or finding a solution strategy for a mathematical problem. The table below summarizes teacher and student actions that embrace struggle as a natural aspect of learning in the mathematics classroom.

Support productive struggle in learning mathematics Teacher and student actions	
What are *teachers* doing?	**What are *students* doing?**
Anticipating what students might struggle with during a lesson and being prepared to support them productively through the struggle.	Struggling at times with mathematics tasks but knowing that breakthroughs often emerge from confusion and struggle.
Giving students time to struggle with tasks, and asking questions that scaffold students' thinking without stepping in to do the work for them.	Asking questions that are related to the sources of their struggles and will help them make progress in understanding and solving tasks.
Helping students realize that confusion and errors are a natural part of learning, by facilitating discussions on mistakes, misconceptions, and struggles.	Persevering in solving problems and realizing that is acceptable to say, "I don't know how to proceed here," but it is not acceptable to give up.
Praising students for their efforts in making sense of mathematical ideas and perseverance in reasoning through problems.	Helping one another without telling their classmates what the answer is or how to solve the problem.

Elicit and Use Evidence of Student Thinking

Effective teaching of mathematics uses evidence of student thinking to assess progress toward mathematical understanding and to adjust instruction continually in ways that support and extend learning.

Effective mathematics teaching elicits evidence of students' current mathematical understanding and uses it as the basis for making instructional decisions. This attention to both eliciting and using evidence is an essential component of formative assessment (Wiliam 2007a). Leahy and colleagues (2005) noted that "teachers using assessment for learning continually look for ways in which they can generate evidence of student learning, and they use this evidence to adapt their instruction to better meet their students' learning needs" (p. 23). A focus on evidence includes identifying indicators of what is important to notice in students' mathematical thinking, planning for ways to elicit that information, interpreting what the evidence means with respect to students' learning, and then deciding how to respond on the basis of students' understanding (Jacobs, Lamb, and Philipp 2010; Sleep and Boerst 2010; van Es 2010).

Discussion

A focus on evidence begins with a clear understanding of what counts as an indicator of students' mathematical thinking (Chamberlin 2005; Sherin and van Es 2003) and requires that teachers attend to more than just whether an answer is or is not correct (Crespo 2000). One source for identifying critical indicators of student thinking is learning trajectories that describe how students' mathematical understanding develops over time (Clements and Sarama 2004; Sztajn et al. 2012). Another source for defining what counts as evidence is common patterns of reasoning that appear in students' thinking, including common difficulties, mistakes, and misconceptions (Swan 2001).

For example, in planning for the task about chairs for the band concert, presented in figure 10, Mr. Harris creates a list of key indicators to notice in his students' work. Specifically, he plans to look for strategies that decompose groups or use the distributive property. He also plans to listen to learn whether students are precise in using concept-based language in discussing their reasoning, such as breaking apart and putting together groups.

The gathering of evidence should neither be left to chance nor occur sporadically. Preparation of each lesson needs to include intentional and systematic plans to elicit evidence that will provide "a constant stream of information about how student learning is evolving toward the desired goal" (Heritage 2008, p. 6). Waiting until the quiz on Friday or the unit test to find out whether students are making adequate progress is too late. Rather, it is important to identify and address potential learning gaps and misconceptions when it matters most to students, which is during instruction, before errors or faulty reasoning becomes consolidated and more difficult to remediate.

Teachers can identify strategic points in each lesson and then plan ways to "check in" on student thinking. One approach is to use high-level tasks to reveal students' thinking and reasoning. For example, tasks that require students to explain, represent, and justify mathematical understanding and skills provide stronger evidence of their understanding for ongoing assessment and instructional decisions. Another approach is to carefully construct key questions, prior to teaching, to draw out specific understandings, conceptual gaps, or common errors, with the goal of making them visible and accessible for examination and discussion (Bray 2013; Swan 2001; Schifter 2001). For example, in the "focusing" pattern of questions that figure 16 shows for the Coin Circulation task, the teacher asked, "Would I be correct if I said a fifty-cent piece would probably be no more than 19 years old?" The teacher has prepared this question to elicit students' understanding of the relationship between random samples and generalizability. The teacher might have also elicited useful evidence from more students by having them turn and talk with a partner about the question prior to the whole-class discussion or having all the students respond to it in writing and handing in their responses for further analysis after the lesson.

Finally, teachers must consider how to interpret and respond to what students say, draw, build, or write, as well as attend to the absence of specific evidence. Jacobs and Ambrose (2008) provide several suggestions for ways that teachers might respond to student thinking. For example, to support students, teachers can ask students to restate a problem in their own words, change the problem to use easier numbers, or, when students are unsuccessful with a specific strategy, remind them of other strategies or tools that they have used in the past. To extend student thinking, teachers can have students compare and contrast strategies, try a more advanced strategy to solve the same problem, or solve similar problems with numbers strategically selected to promote more sophisticated strategies. Although there is no single best way to respond to student thinking, the response that the teacher gives should be intended to help students deepen their conceptual understanding while moving them forward, toward procedural fluency and advanced mathematical reasoning.

Illustration

Figure 22 illustrates ways in which how Ms. Lewis, a first-grade teacher, elicits and uses evidence of student thinking. Having noticed that some students seem unsure of the meaning of the equal sign as a symbol of equality, Ms. Lewis wonders whether this uncertainty might be prevalent among her other students as well. Her learning goal for the lesson that the figure shows is to help her students understand more clearly that the equal sign indicates that quantities or expressions "have the same value." Ms. Lewis observes her students' different solutions and strategies in their work and probes some of the students' thinking to learn more about their reasoning, and she uses this information to make adjustments to her instruction.

Consider how Ms. Lewis uses the evidence of her students' thinking throughout the lesson to adjust her instruction in ways that support students in engaging in mathematical discourse about equality and the meaning of the equal sign. In particular, notice how Gabe's thinking about the "number of the day" routine influences both the decisions of the teacher and the reasoning of the students. Then note how Ms. Lewis uses a writing prompt to gather further evidence on what each student understands by the end of the lesson.

Ms. Lewis begins the lesson by asking all the students to work on their own to solve the problem $8 + 4 = \square + 7$. As the students work, she takes note of the different solutions and strategies in their work and probes some of the students' thinking to learn more about their reasoning.

Ms. Lewis notices several different answers, including 12, 5, 19, 11, and 6, so she asks the students to find someone in the class with an answer that is different from their own and compare and discuss their solutions. The conversation is lively as students wonder how there can possibly be so many different answers and whether any of them is even correct. Some students even change their answers as a result of their conversations.

After a few minutes, Ms. Lewis asks the students to bring their papers to the rug so that they can discuss the work as a class. Ms. Lewis asks Maddie to share her work first (shown below on the left). Maddie explains that she didn't know what to do with the 7. The class affirms that the sum of 8 and 4 is 12, and they agree that this fact seems to be an important thing to know in solving the problem.

Gabe presents his work next (shown below on the right). He explains that he thought the total had to be the same on both sides of the equal sign, so he used his drawing to figure out that 5 will make both sides total 12. Ms. Lewis asks him to explain why he thought it might be true that both sides have to have the same total. He said that he thought about how they sometimes write equations that only have one number on the left, like 5 = 2 + 3, or when they write the "number of the day" in different ways without using an equal sign at all. The teacher asks the other students to comment on these ideas. Alex adds that they write the number of the day in different ways to name that number, and he suggests that this case might be something like that. Ms. Lewis asks all the students to turn and talk with a partner about how this task might relate to their previous work when 12 was the number of the day.

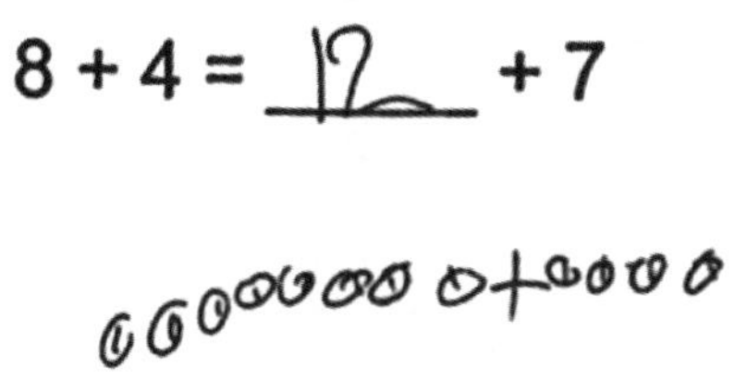

Maddie's work 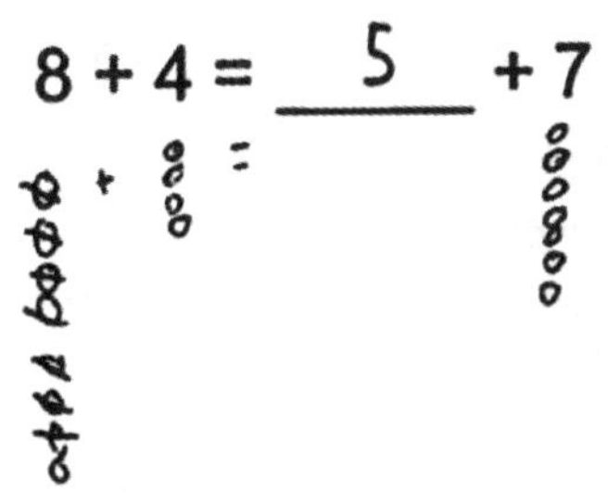   Gabe's work

Fig. 22. Ms. Lewis's eliciting and use of student thinking on
the meaning of the equal sign

After some more whole-class discussion, Ms. Lewis asks all the students to return to their seats and take out a piece of paper. She asks them to make up a similar problem on their own and use it to complete this sentence starter, "The equal sign means that _____." The students find partners to review their work, then they make revisions to it, and finally the teacher collects the work to analyze it further and consider her next instructional steps.

Fig. 22. *Continued*

Teacher and student actions

Effective teaching involves finding the mathematics in students' comments and actions, considering what students appear to know in light of the intended learning goals and progression, and determining how to give the best response and support to students on the basis of their current understandings. Teachers also use the evidence gathered after the instructional session to reflect on the lesson and student progress and then identify next steps in planning future lessons and designing interventions. The actions in the table below summarize what teachers and students are doing in mathematics classrooms that use evidence of student thinking to assess, support, and extend learning.

Elicit and use evidence of student thinking	
Teacher and student actions	
What are *teachers* doing?	**What are *students* doing?**
Identifying what counts as evidence of student progress toward mathematics learning goals.	Revealing their mathematical understanding, reasoning, and methods in written work and classroom discourse.
Eliciting and gathering evidence of student understanding at strategic points during instruction.	Reflecting on mistakes and misconceptions to improve their mathematical understanding.
Interpreting student thinking to assess mathematical understanding, reasoning, and methods.	Asking questions, responding to, and giving suggestions to support the learning of their classmates.
Making in-the-moment decisions on how to respond to students with questions and prompts that probe, scaffold, and extend.	Assessing and monitoring their own progress toward mathematics learning goals and identifying areas in which they need to improve.
Reflecting on evidence of student learning to inform the planning of next instructional steps.	

Moving to action

Although the important work of teaching is not limited to the eight Mathematics Teaching Practices discussed in this chapter, this core set of research-informed practices is offered as a framework for strengthening the teaching and learning of mathematics. The next steps involve educators in collectively and collaboratively supporting one another in moving toward improved instruction through the lens of these core teaching practices. Effective teaching of mathematics begins with teachers clarifying and understanding the mathematics that students need to learn and how it develops along learning progressions. The establishment of clear goals supports the selection of tasks that promote reasoning and problem solving while developing conceptual understanding and procedural fluency. With effective teaching, the classroom is rich in mathematical discourse among students in using and making connections among mathematical representations as they compare and analyze varied solution strategies. The teacher carefully facilitates this discourse with purposeful questioning. Teachers acknowledge the value of productive struggle in learning mathematics, and they support students in developing a disposition to persevere in solving problems. They guide their teaching and learning interactions by evidence of student thinking so that they can assess and advance student reasoning and sense making about important mathematical ideas and relationships.

Essential Elements

The Mathematics Teaching Practices described and illustrated in the previous section support effective learning for all students. However, although such teaching and learning form the nonnegotiable core of successful mathematics programs, they are part of a system of essential elements of excellent mathematics programs. Consistent implementation of effective teaching and learning of mathematics, as previously described in the eight Mathematics Teaching Practices, are possible only when school mathematics programs have in place—

- a commitment to **access and equity**;
- a powerful **curriculum**;
- appropriate **tools and technology**;
- meaningful and aligned **assessment**; and
- a culture of **professionalism**.

This section describes and illustrates each of these five essential elements of effective school mathematics programs.

Access and Equity

An excellent mathematics program requires that all students have access to a high-quality mathematics curriculum, effective teaching and learning, high expectations, and the support and resources needed to maximize their learning potential.

Equity does not mean that every student should receive identical instruction; instead, it demands that reasonable and appropriate accommodations be made as needed to promote access and attainment for all students. (NCTM 2000, p. 12)

Often, inequalities in achievement are perceived as the result of a hierarchy of competence. When the very students who have been given more opportunities to learn show higher achievement than students provided fewer opportunities to learn, they are perceived as more capable or having more aptitude. This manner of talking about achievement gaps without mentioning opportunity gaps that cause them invites a focus on deficit models to "explain" low performance in terms of factors such as cultural differences, poverty, low levels of parental education, and so on. (Flores 2007, p. 40)

Access and equity in mathematics at the school and classroom levels rest on beliefs and practices that empower all students to participate meaningfully in learning mathematics and to achieve outcomes in mathematics that are not predicted by or correlated with student characteristics. These outcomes include performance on mathematics assessments, disposition toward mathematics, persistence in mathematics coursework, and the ability to use mathematics in authentic contexts (Gutiérrez 2002). Support for access and equity requires, but is not limited to, high expectations, access to high-quality mathematics curriculum and instruction, adequate time for students to learn, appropriate emphasis on differentiated processes that broaden students' productive engagement with mathematics, and human and material resources.

Equity in school mathematics outcomes is often conflated with *equality* of inputs. Providing all students the same curricular materials, the same methods of teaching, the same amount of instructional time, and the same school-based supports for learning is different from ensuring that all students, regardless of background characteristics, have the same likelihood of achieving meaningful outcomes (Gutiérrez 2013).

Our vision of access and equity requires being responsive to students' backgrounds, experiences and knowledge when designing, implementing, and assessing the effectiveness of a mathematics program. Acknowledging and addressing factors that contribute to differential outcomes among groups of students is critical to ensure that all students routinely have opportunities to experience high-quality mathematics instruction, learn challenging mathematics content, and receive the support necessary to be successful. Our vision of equity and access includes both ensuring that all students attain mathematics proficiency and increasing the numbers of students from all racial, ethnic, gender, and socioeconomic groups who attain the highest levels of mathematics achievement.

Attending to access and equity also means recognizing that mathematics programs that have served some groups of students, in effect privileging some students over others, must be critically examined and enhanced, if needed, to ensure that they meet the needs of *all* students. That is, they must serve students who are black, Latino/a, American Indian, or members of other minorities, as well as those who are considered to be white; students who are female as well as those who are male; students of poverty as well as those of wealth; students who are English language learners as well as those for whom English is their first language; students who have not been successful in school and in mathematics as well as those who have succeeded; and students whose parents have had limited access to educational opportunities as well as those whose parents have had ample educational opportunities. Moreover, attending to access and equity means recognizing that inequitable learning opportunities can exist in any setting, diverse or homogenous, whenever only some, but not all, teachers implement rigorous curricula or use the Mathematics Teaching Practices described earlier.

Abundant research has documented the significant outcomes that are possible when schools and teachers systematically address obstacles to success in mathematics for students from historically underserved populations (Boaler 1997, 2006; Boaler and Staples 2008; Campbell 1996; Cross et al. 2012; Gutiérrez 2000; Kisker et. al. 2012; Knapp et al. 1995; Lipka et al. 2007; McKenzie et al. 2011). The question is not whether all students can succeed in mathematics but whether the adults organizing mathematics learning opportunities can alter traditional beliefs and practices to promote success for all.

Obstacles

A range of obstacles exists to making significant progress in achieving the Access and Equity Principle. One of these involves the quality of instruction available to students. Researchers have consistently found that students living in poverty, whether urban or rural, as well as students who have struggled to learn mathematics, are more likely to have teachers who have weaker mathematics backgrounds, less professional experience, and certification outside of rather than in mathematics, and who are perceived to be less effective (Battey 2013; Darling-Hammond 2007; Flores 2007; Stiff, Johnson, and Akos 2011). Moreover, in instruction for these students, the Mathematics Teaching Practices described previously are rarely implemented consistently to support meaningful learning. Instead, lessons commonly focus primarily on rote skills and procedures, with scant attention to meaningful mathematics learning (Ellis 2008; Ellis and Berry 2005).

Another obstacle to access and equity involves differential opportunities to learn high-quality grade-level mathematics content and to be held to high expectations for mathematics achievement (Jackson et al. 2013; Phelps et al. 2012; Walker 2003). This often occurs as a result of tracking, or separating students academically on the basis of presumed ability—an unquestioned or commonly tolerated policy that is found in over 85 percent of U.S. schools and limits participation and achievement for students (Biafora and Ansalone 2008). Tracking consigns some students to mathematical content that offers little significant mathematical substance (Burris et al. 2008). While some students are expected to engage in a variety of mathematics topics through multiple teaching and learning strategies, students in low tracks are often confronted with a narrow and fragmented mathematics curriculum, delivered with a limited set of teaching and learning strategies (Ellis 2008; Tate and Rousseau 2002). Too often, because of the unproductive beliefs described below, the capacities of so-called low-track students are underestimated, leading to these students receiving fewer opportunities to learn challenging mathematics. Low-track students encounter a vicious cycle of low expectations: Because little is expected of them, they exert little effort, their halfhearted efforts reinforce low expectations, and the result is low achievement (Gamoran 2011).

Advocates of tracking argue that it assists mathematics teaching and learning by matching students' ability levels to an appropriate curriculum (Schmidt, Cogan, and Houang 2011). The assumption that underlies this belief is that creating different tracks is an effective strategy to accommodate differences in students' needs. The belief is that tracking eases the challenges of teaching by narrowing the range of student differences so that instructional practices can be targeted to a narrower set of student needs. Implicit in this belief is the idea that students in low-level and high-level tracks would receive few, if any, benefits from being in the same learning environment.

Although some research supports grouping gifted and talented students in homogeneous groups to maximize their learning (Delcourt et al. 1994), research also shows that the learning of students assigned to lower-ability groups is depressed, regardless of their ability levels (Stiff, Johnson, and Akos 2011). In addition, once students are placed in low-level or "slow" math groups, they are very likely to remain in those groups until they leave school (Boaler 2008; Ellis 2008). When middle-level students thought to be "at risk" in mathematics are placed in grade-level mathematics courses and provided the support necessary to be successful in those courses, their achievement gains are greater, and they are more likely to enroll in upper-level math courses in the following years, than when they are placed in lower-ability math courses (Boaler and Staples 2008; Burris, Heubert, and Levin 2006). Further, evidence suggests that high-achieving students in heterogeneous classes are not statistically different from homogeneously tracked students in achievement and participation in Advanced Placement (AP) mathematics courses (Burris, Heubert, and Levin 2006; Staples 2008).

Eliminating low-level tracks does not mean eliminating Advanced Placement or more rigorous high school courses. An effective mathematics program supports and challenges students who have demonstrated strong interest and achievement in mathematics as well as those who have not. However, offering two levels of high school courses, both featuring high-quality curriculum and instruction, is very different from the typical practice of offering multiple levels of the same course (e.g., Algebra 1, Applied Algebra, Algebra 1 Honors, Introductory Algebra, First-Year Fundamental Algebra) with different curricula and expectations (Schmidt, Cogan, and McKnight, 2010). Further, when mathematics programs offer advanced courses, they must ensure that pathways to the highest-level courses exist for all students, along with the support to encourage their participation and success.

Even more disturbing is the lack of self-confidence that far too many students develop and that leads them to view mathematics as something that is far beyond their grasp and that they can never hope to understand. They see mathematics as being within the reach of only a few exceptional "mathematical geniuses." Parents may unwittingly reinforce this notion by excusing low performance by their children as genetic destiny (saying, for example, "I was never any good at math, either"). Furthermore, educators may reinforce this misconception by sorting students by ability, believing that some can "do math" and others cannot.

These obstacles are seldom, if ever, erected purposely to limit the participation or achievement of groups of students. Rather, they emerge in part from a set of beliefs, summarized in the table below, which must be acknowledged and discussed openly. It is important to note that these beliefs should not be viewed as good or bad, but rather as productive when they lead to change and promote equity or unproductive when they limit student access to important mathematics content and practices. Until unproductive beliefs are confronted, it is unlikely that the goal of mathematical success for all students will be achieved.

The following table compares some unproductive and productive beliefs that influence the access that students have to effective instruction, high-quality curriculum, and differentiated learning supports.

Beliefs about access and equity in mathematics	
Unproductive beliefs	**Productive beliefs**
Students possess different innate levels of ability in mathematics, and these cannot be changed by instruction. Certain groups or individuals have it while others do not.	Mathematics ability is a function of opportunity, experience, and effort—not of innate intelligence. Mathematics teaching and learning cultivate mathematics abilities. All students are capable of participating and achieving in mathematics, and all deserve support to achieve at the highest levels.
Equity is the same as equality. All students need to receive the same learning opportunities so that they can achieve the same academic outcomes.	Equity is attained when students receive the differentiated supports (e.g., time, instruction, curricular materials, programs) necessary to ensure that all students are mathematically successful.
Equity is only an issue for schools with racial and ethnic diversity or significant numbers of low-income students.	Equity—ensuring that all students have access to high-quality curriculum, instruction, and the supports that they need to be successful—applies to all settings.
Students who are not fluent in the English language are less able to learn mathematics and therefore must be in a separate track for English language learners (ELLs).	Students who are not fluent in English can learn the language of mathematics at grade level or beyond at the same time that they are learning English when appropriate instructional strategies are used.
Mathematics learning is independent of students' culture, conditions, and language, and teachers do not need to consider any of these factors to be effective.	Effective mathematics instruction leverages students' culture, conditions, and language to support and enhance mathematics learning.
Students living in poverty lack the cognitive, emotional, and behavioral characteristics to participate and achieve in mathematics.	Effective teaching practices (e.g., engaging students with challenging tasks, discourse, and open-ended problem solving) have the potential to open up greater opportunities for higher-order thinking and for raising the mathematics achievement of all students, including poor and low-income students.

Beliefs about access and equity in mathematics, *continued*	
Unproductive beliefs	**Productive beliefs**
Tracking promotes students' achievement by allowing students to be placed in "homogeneous" classes and groups where they can make the greatest learning gains.	The practice of isolating low-achieving students in low-level or slower-paced mathematics groups should be eliminated.
Only high-achieving or gifted students can reason about, make sense of, and persevere in solving challenging mathematics problems.	All students are capable of making sense of and persevering in solving challenging mathematics problems and should be expected to do so. Many more students, regardless of gender, ethnicity, and socioeconomic status, need to be given the support, confidence, and opportunities to reach much higher levels of mathematical success and interest.

Overcoming the obstacles

Achieving equity with respect to student learning outcomes will require that educators at all levels operate with the belief that all students can learn. Closing existing learning gaps requires ensuring that all students have access to high-quality instruction, a challenging curriculum, exciting extracurricular opportunities, and the differentiated supports and enrichment that are necessary to promote student success at continually increasing levels.

Beliefs and expectations

To ensure that all students have access to an equitable mathematics program, educators need to identify, acknowledge, and discuss the mindsets and beliefs that they have about students' abilities. Fixed mindsets (i.e., the attitude that levels of mathematics ability are fixed and cannot be changed), when coupled with societal stereotypes about academic ability that are based on student characteristics, perpetuate the unproductive practices described above (Dweck 2008). In contrast, a growth mindset, which emphasizes mathematics teaching and learning as processes that cultivate mathematical abilities, stresses that success and learning are a reflection of effort and not intelligence alone, and thus promotes a belief that all students are capable of participating and achieving in mathematics (Boaler 2011; Dweck 2006).

Believing in, and acting on, growth mindsets versus fixed mindsets can make an enormous difference in what students accomplish. Setting and acting on high expectations and a genuine belief that student effort and effective instruction outweigh "smarts" and circumstances increase students' opportunities to learn. Teachers with fixed mindsets can unfairly justify differential allocation of resources and opportunities on the basis of students' prior academic achievement, abilities, or interests. Research has found that a fixed mindset is strongly correlated with socioeconomic background, contributes to widening opportunity gaps, and reinforces inequities (Dweck 2008; Gamoran 2010). To address this obstacle, teachers should promote and display a growth mindset at all times. A growth mindset values all students' thinking and uses pedagogical practices such as differentiated tasks, mixed-ability groupings, and public praise for contributions and perseverance to cultivate mathematical participation and achievement (Boaler 2011).

Promoting student engagement (by, e.g., selecting challenging tasks, exerting intense effort and concentration in the implementation of tasks), framing mathematics within the growth mindset, acknowledging student contributions, and attending to culture and language play substantial roles in equalizing mathematics gains between poor and non-poor students (Battey 2013; Cross et al. 2012; Kisker et al. 2012; Robinson 2013). Furthermore, increasing access of poor and low-income students to teaching that effectively enacts the Mathematics Teaching Practices described earlier has the potential to open up greater opportunities for higher-order thinking and for raising the intellectual quality of student cognition (Boaler and Staples 2008; Burris et al. 2008; Lubienski 2007).

With a systemic commitment to all students and expectations that all students can meet or exceed grade-level standards for mathematics, educators can more easily move away from past practices, such as tracking that separated students, and instead develop productive practices that support learning for all.

Curriculum and instruction

When differences in ability, background, and interest arise, as they always will, more effective instruction and differentiated supports can overcome the obstacles discussed above. Policies that boost and supplement learning, provide additional time, and give students access to a rigorous curriculum and teachers who implement a range of approaches and resources are far more likely to raise achievement than policies that relegate students who have traditionally underperformed to dead-end tracks with an unchallenging curriculum.

Persistent and unacceptable gaps narrow and ultimately disappear when all students have access to rigorous, high-quality mathematics, taught by teachers who not only understand mathematics but also understand and appreciate learners' social and cultural contexts in meaningful ways. Effective teachers draw on community resources to understand how they can use contexts, culture, conditions, and language to support mathematics teaching and learning (Berry and Ellis 2013; Cross et al. 2012; Kisker et al. 2012; Moschkovich 1999, 2011; Planas and Civil 2013). As a result, learning mathematics becomes a part of a student's sense of identity, leading to increased engagement and motivation in mathematics (Aguirre, Mayfield-Ingram, and Martin 2013; Boaler 1997; Hogan 2008; Middleton and Jansen 2011).

Classroom environments that foster a sense of community that allows students to express their mathematical ideas—together with norms that expect students to communicate their mathematical thinking to their peers and teacher, both orally and in writing, using the language of mathematics—positively affect participation and engagement among all students (Horn 2012; Webel 2010). All students, including ELLs, can learn mathematics content at the same time that they are learning the academic language of mathematics, both in English and in symbols (Razfar, Khisty, and Chval 2011). The language of mathematics provides an opportunity for many students, including ELLs, to show their prior preparation and to help one another in the language that they have in common—the language of mathematics (Moschkovich 1999, 2011).

Furthermore, a focus on the mathematical practices outlined in CCSSM can benefit students at all levels by engaging them in doing mathematics in ways that make sense to them. Rather than imposing a standard algorithm or a set solution strategy, students can devise their own strategies that are more meaningful to them, easier to remember, or culturally familiar (Carpenter et al. 1989). Particularly useful in this endeavor are problems that have multiple entry points and allow for the use of a broad range of strategies or approaches. More advanced students can extend their thinking as they work with problems with multiple entry points, while less advanced students, including students with disabilities, have opportunities to continue to develop basic understandings that they need to move forward (Dieker et al. 2011). Moreover, problems that students can enter and reason about at multiple levels can accommodate a range of learning styles and cultural backgrounds.

Interventions and support personnel

Supporting the success of all students requires having an effective intervention program in place to address learning difficulties as soon as they occur. Although specific program design features will vary by level and other factors, effective intervention programs should—

- be mandatory, not optional (i.e., scheduled during the school day whenever possible);
- be based on constant monitoring of students' progress, as determined from the results of formative and summative assessment, ensuring that students get support as quickly as possible;
- attend to conceptual understanding as well as procedural fluency; and
- allow for flexible movement in and out of the intervention as students need it (Kanold and Larson 2012).

One option is to provide such intervention during regular mathematics instructional time. For example, elementary teachers of the same grade may decide to schedule their ninety-minute math block at the same time so that they can use the first twenty minutes of each period for mathematics intervention—with students regrouped across classes according to their learning needs and then returning to their heterogeneous class for the regular mathematics lesson.

Another option is to allocate additional time outside the grade-level mathematics course during which students with learning gaps can receive specific, targeted support (Burris et al. 2008; Rubin and Noguera 2004). These additional learning opportunities should enable these students to explore math on a deep, intriguing, innovative level. These sessions might be offered during a "double-dose" math time as well as outside the regular school day. In addition to regular curricular support, engaging co-curricular and extracurricular opportunities, such as mathematics clubs, circles, and competitions, as well as access to mentors, can help students achieve the highest levels of mathematical passion, creativity, and expertise, regardless of gender, ethnicity, or socioeconomic status. These resources should enable students not only to see beyond math simply as a school subject, but also to appreciate the beauty, wonder, utility, and vitality of mathematics at a deep level, helping them to incorporate it into their future high-level decision making.

Another strategy for promoting equitable, full access to opportunities to learn mathematics is the deployment of instructional support personnel (for example, mathematics resource teachers, intervention teachers, or gifted specialists) who can provide specialized support services to schools and teachers or can work directly with students who are either underperforming or exceeding grade-level standards of proficiency or who display curiosity and desire for learning additional mathematics. Schools serving learners in diverse contexts with diverse learning needs can use the assistance of school-based mathematics coaches and specialists to enhance teachers' abilities and capacities to meet individual students' learning needs, improve instruction, and monitor students' progress. Mathematics coaches and specialists can positively influence teachers' beliefs about mathematics teaching and learning and increase teachers' participation in non-coaching professional activities, such as attending mathematics-focused grade-level meetings, observing peers' teaching, or attending schoolwide mathematics workshops (Campbell and Malkus 2011).

Illustration

The following example illustrates an intervention at the high school level to ensure that all students continue to move forward, learning challenging, high-level mathematics:

> Teachers and administrators at a high school in a mid-Atlantic state became aware that a significant number of ninth graders were not succeeding in Algebra 1. To deal with this concern, the mathematics teachers and the school administrators began meeting regularly to brainstorm about ways to address this inequity. In reviewing the records of these students, they found that the correlation between the students' achievement on the eighth-grade state assessment and their performance in Algebra 1 in ninth grade was extremely high. The teachers concluded that many of these students were likely to have gaps in their knowledge that prevented them from achieving to their fullest potential when they took Algebra 1.

To address this problem, the school designed a new course, Algebra Seminar, for approximately 20 percent of its ninth-grade students—primarily those scoring at a "basic" or "below basic" level on the eighth-grade assessment and therefore deemed unlikely to pass the Algebra 1 end-of-course exam if they enrolled in a typical one-period Algebra 1 class. To ensure that the students in this course would receive the appropriate levels of support, the principal agreed to schedule common planning time for Algebra Seminar teachers so that they could collaboratively design the course, plan lessons, and enhance pedagogical practices.

Multiple design features of the new Algebra Seminar course make it an effective intervention that meets the vision of the Access and Equity Principle. The new course—

- teaches Algebra 1 course content along with critical prerequisite content, with a "just-in-time" approach to prerequisite content;

- is team-taught by a mathematics teacher and a special education teacher to ensure that the special needs students who are mainstreamed into the class receive the additional support that they need to succeed;

- is systematically planned as a back-to-back double period (ninety minutes a day);

- is capped at eighteen students, so that teachers have the opportunity to address individual students' needs;

- is enriched by focused professional development for the teachers;

- uses a broad array of print and non-print, and basal and supplemental, resources;

- engages students and enhances instruction with a variety of tools and technology, including interactive whiteboards, graphing calculators, tablet computers, response clickers, and a range of manipulative materials;

- incorporates a wide variety of highly effective instructional practices that reflect the Mathematics Teaching Practices; and

- draws on online lesson plans and other resources that teachers use to initiate their planning.

As a result of this comprehensive and well-designed intervention, Algebra Seminar students consistently catch up and perform as well as the single-period Algebra 1 students on the end-of-course Algebra 1 exam and are prepared to enroll in a regular geometry course the following year.

Moving to action

To provide access and equity, teachers go beyond "good teaching," to teaching that ensures that all students have opportunities to engage successfully in the mathematics classroom and learn challenging mathematics. Making this Principle a reality requires all stakeholders to monitor the extent to which all students have access to a challenging mathematics curriculum, taught by skilled and effective teachers who know and understand the cultures and communities from which their students come and who also use this knowledge to create meaningful tasks that build on students' prior knowledge and experiences. These teachers also monitor student progress and make needed accommodations. To do this effectively, they work collaboratively with colleagues, including teachers of special education, gifted education, and English language learners, as well as families and community members, to ensure that all students have the support that they need to maximize their success in the mathematics classroom. Further, teachers need to collaborate with one another to implement the Mathematics Teaching Practices outlined earlier and promote a growth mindset in their classrooms and school.

Finally, district and school policies must be reviewed to ensure that systemic practices are not disadvantaging particular groups or subgroups of students on the basis of societal stereotypes. This analysis should include a review of tracking, student placement, opportunities for both remediation and enrichment, and student outcomes, including persistence in the mathematics pipeline.

Curriculum

An excellent mathematics program includes a curriculum that develops important mathematics along coherent learning progressions and develops connections among areas of mathematical study and between mathematics and the real world.

What is meant by *curriculum*? In many cases, educators and community members use the terms *curriculum* and *textbooks* interchangeably, just as many often collapse the distinction between *standards* and *curriculum*. *Standards* are statements of what students are expected to learn. Standards are the *ends*. A *curriculum* is the program used to help students meet the standards, including instructional materials, activities, tasks, units, lessons, and assessments. The curriculum is the *means*.

Standards should be designed with intended learning progressions (or trajectories) across the pre-K–12 spectrum and beyond. The design of a curriculum implies a "sequence of thoughts, ways of reasoning, and strategies that a student employs when learning a topic" (Battista 2011). For example, in CCSSM, mathematical ideas build developmentally year by year on what came before, with students making connections to prior topics while laying a foundation for future learning (Daro, Mosher, and Corcoran 2011). Consequently, curricula based on CCSSM should be designed so that students and teachers can make mathematical connections across content topics that capitalize on CCSSM's underlying structure, so that, for example, students can appreciate the use of a geometric model when exploring a number pattern or the use of ratios when analyzing a probability problem. The broad view of learning progressions in any set of college- and career-ready standards must guide both the work of schools and districts in developing curricular frameworks and other instructional resources and the efforts of developers of textbooks and other instructional materials.

Mathematics curricula can be characterized from both a horizontal and a vertical perspective. From a horizontal perspective, teachers need an in-depth understanding of the mathematics and materials that they use to teach a particular course or grade level. From this perspective, fourth-grade teachers need a deep understanding of all the content to be addressed that year, the concepts and skills that need to be taught, how the topics connect with one another, how the mathematics content is sequenced, how much time might be needed for each topic, what tools (such as textbooks, materials, and technology) are available to support the content, and how to assess student understanding of the fourth-grade content standards.

From a vertical perspective, fourth-grade teachers need to understand what the students have learned in the past, how this year's curriculum builds on students' prior knowledge and experiences, and how the mathematics content that is studied this year will lay the foundation for topics that students will explore in fifth grade and beyond. A vertical understanding of the curriculum helps teachers engage in dialogue with colleagues who teach in grade levels below or above their own grade level (or with colleagues who teach the previous or the next course in a high school sequence) so that they can examine strengths and weaknesses of the overall program to prioritize the needs of students.

Obstacles

Content included in textbooks influences what is taught and emphasized by teachers in the classroom (Schmidt, Houang, and Cohen 2002; Tarr et al. 2006). Some textbooks are effectively organized to focus on big mathematical ideas, such as those outlined in CCSSM and state or provincial standards, and to emphasize connections among topics. Unfortunately, others are less effectively organized, and schools often place too much emphasis on adhering to the content and sequence of such materials. Moreover, some teachers' lack of deep understanding of the content that they are expected to teach may inhibit their ability to teach meaningful, effective, and connected lesson sequences, regardless of the materials that they have available.

Grade-level mathematics content standards are too often treated as checklists of topics. When they are regarded in this light, mathematics content becomes nothing more than a set of isolated skills, often without a mathematical or real-world context and disconnected from related topics. A typical traditional high school mathematics course sequence that spends a year on algebra, a year on geometry, and another year on algebra frequently focuses on covering a list of topics rather than on presenting a coherent program that "uncovers" those topics, establishing connections among them throughout the three years. Similar effects can be seen in other grades when the school year is organized into disjointed units addressing different domains of mathematics.

Even with the best curriculum model, lesson planning in some classrooms is conducted on a day-to-day basis, blindly sequenced by sections in a textbook, with little attention to the broader curriculum, contextual applications of the mathematics, or progressions of the topics and how they fit together. Furthermore, curriculum maps and pacing guides often dictate the topic, and sometimes even the page number of a book, to be addressed on each day of the school year, without regard for differences among students and classes. Teachers using pacing guides tend to feel rushed and, as a result, they often omit rich and challenging problem-solving tasks that are essential for developing deeper mathematical understanding (David and Greene 2007).

The table on the next page compares some unproductive and productive beliefs that influence the implementation of an effective curriculum. It is important to note that these beliefs should not be viewed as good or bad, but rather as productive when they support effective teaching and learning or unproductive when they limit student access to important mathematics content and practices.

Beliefs about the mathematics curriculum	
Unproductive beliefs	**Productive beliefs**
The content and sequence of topics in a textbook always define the curriculum. Everything included in the textbook is important and should always be addressed, and what is not in the book is not important.	Standards should drive decisions about which topics to address and which to omit in the curriculum. How a textbook is used depends on its quality—i.e., the degree to which it provides coherent, balanced instruction in content aligned with standards and provides lessons that consistently support implementation of the Mathematics Teaching Practices.
Knowing the mathematics curriculum for a particular grade level or course is sufficient to effectively teach the content to students.	Mathematics teachers need to have a clear understanding of the curriculum within and across grade levels—in other words, student learning progressions—to effectively teach a particular grade level or course in the sequence.
Implementation of a pacing guide ensures that teachers address all the required topics and guarantees continuity so that all students are studying the same topics on the same days.	Curriculum maps and pacing guides attempt to ensure coverage of content but do not guarantee that students learn the mathematics. Adequate time to provide for meaningful learning, differentiation, and interventions must be provided for students to develop deep understanding of the content.
Mathematics is a static, unchanging field.	Mathematics is a dynamic field that is ever changing. Emphases in the curriculum are evolving, and it is important to embrace and adapt to appropriate changes.
The availability of open-source mathematics curricula means that every teacher should design his or her own curriculum and textbook.	Open-source curricula are resources to be examined collaboratively and used to support the established learning progressions of a coherent and effective mathematics program.

Overcoming the obstacles

A mathematics curriculum is more than a collection of activities; instead it is a coherent sequencing of core mathematical ideas that are well articulated within and across grades and courses. Such curricula pose problems that promote conceptual understanding, problem solving, and reasoning and are drawn from contexts in everyday life and other subjects.

Designing standards and curriculum

In light of the sheer quantity of mathematics that could be addressed in any grade or course, it is important to make careful choices about what specific mathematics to include. Those designing curriculum standards and related documents need to carefully consider whether topics remain in the curriculum because of tradition, or, more important, whether they are necessary in promoting students' readiness for college, careers, and life. Some topics may warrant increased attention, given their prevalence in students' future use of mathematics in postsecondary study or the workplace. For example, as NCTM argued in *Focus in High School Mathematics* (2009), statistics is increasingly recognized as essential for students' success in dealing with the requirements of citizenship, employment, and continuing education (Franklin et al. 2007; College Board 2006; American Diploma Project 2004). Likewise, discrete mathematics, algorithmic thinking, and mathematical modeling may warrant additional attention, given their importance in computer science and related fields. Mathematical curricula also need to reflect changing emphases within the field of mathematics. As the report *Mathematical Sciences in 2025* (National Research Council 2013a, p. 2) states,

> Mathematical sciences work is becoming an increasingly integral and essential component of a growing array of areas of investigation in biology, medicine, social sciences, business, advanced design, climate, finance, advanced materials, and many more. This work involves the integration of mathematics, statistics, and computation in the broadest sense and the interplay of these areas with areas of potential application.

Finally, curriculum design needs to take into consideration the amount of new content to be introduced in a particular grade or course so that sufficient time will be available to teach concepts and procedures, using the Mathematics Teaching Practices. That is, sufficient time is needed to—

- engage students in tasks that promote problem solving and reasoning to make sense of new mathematical ideas;
- engage students in meaningful mathematical discussions; and
- build fluency with procedures on a foundation of conceptual understanding.

One of the positive features of CCSSM is its focus and coherence in grades K–8 and the delay of expected fluency in standard computational algorithms. These features provide instructional time for students to build conceptual understanding and proficiency in the mathematical practices and to develop fluency in standard computational algorithms that is based on their understanding of properties, operations, and the base-ten number system.

Implementation of curriculum

Teachers who are well prepared in their knowledge of mathematics, students' thinking, and the school's curriculum are positioned to appreciate how mathematical thinking develops over time and are equipped to help students connect topics to strengthen understanding (Ball, Thames, and Phelps 2008). Also, when teachers recognize the importance of developing students' proficiency with the mathematical practices, they can more effectively select and implement appropriate tasks that emphasize mathematical thinking throughout the pre-K–12 years. Instructional materials and tasks selected by schools have a significant influence on what students learn and how they learn it (Stein, Remillard, and Smith 2007). Consequently, teachers need high-quality professional development to maximize the effectiveness of these materials, since even the best textbooks and resources can be misinterpreted or misused.

Given the central role of textbooks as a resource and their potential for supporting instruction, textbook selection should not be taken lightly. This process should consider not only whether textbooks "cover" standards but also whether their development of content reflects learning progressions focused on conceptual understanding and emphasizes the mathematical practices (Bush et al. 2011; NGA Center and CCSSO 2013). As discussed earlier, the Mathematics Teaching Practices promote students' conceptual understanding and proficiency in the mathematical practices. Thus, another important selection criterion is the extent to which a textbook's lessons consistently support these teaching practices.

Appropriate use of textbooks—whether to teach from them lesson-by-lesson almost exclusively or whether to treat them as one resource among many—depends on the quality of the textbook, as defined above. If a textbook develops mathematical topics in a coherent manner, based on learning progressions, and features lessons that consistently support the Mathematics Teaching Practices, then teaching primarily from that textbook makes sense, and significant omissions or deviations can decrease, rather than enhance, the quality of instruction (Banilower et al. 2006). Conversely, if a textbook does not provide such support, then the only option is to treat it as one of many resources and supplement it as needed.

Some schools develop pacing guides to ensure that instruction addresses all the required standards in the school year and spends an appropriate amount of time on each topic. Although these resources can help teachers with long- and short-term planning, the needs of individual classes and students should have priority over rigid curricular schedules. Collaboration among teachers throughout the school year can result in appropriate adjustments and adaptations of pacing guides to address student strengths and weaknesses.

Structuring units—and lessons within the units—around broad mathematical themes or approaches, rather than lists of specific skills, creates coherence that provides students with the foundational knowledge for more robust and meaningful learning of mathematics. In particular, attention to the mathematical practices provides students with important mathematical tools that they need to navigate mathematical situations and contexts. In planning lessons, teachers should also consider the intended standards and the developmental needs of the students. Consequently, careful consideration should be given to appropriate ways to sequence a series of lessons. Daily lesson plans should take into account the broader perspective of what students learned in the past and where they are headed in the future, as well as the contexts that can be used to motivate students and help them understand why particular topics are important.

High school mathematics

Efforts to achieve curricular coherence in mathematics at the high school level are particularly challenging, given the typical sequence of courses and topics, in which the study of geometry is often isolated as a separate course and statistics is grafted onto courses in stand-alone units rather than naturally connected to related topics (e.g., using a visual line of best fit to lead into a formal study of linear functions). Some schools have successfully reconfigured their programs as integrated sequences of courses that address algebra, geometry, statistics, probability, and discrete mathematics topics across all grade levels, allowing students to revisit these topics at increasingly sophisticated levels and make connections among them. Such reconfiguration requires developing mathematical reasoning and helping students see how, for example, a probability problem can be solved by use of a geometric model, or how geometric transformations of shapes can be performed through the use of matrices in algebra.

All high schools should reevaluate their mathematics programs to determine whether the current sequence of courses is preparing students for the demands of a workplace that will require more than the mastery of isolated mathematics skills. Such a reevaluation might require that teachers know "how and why mathematical models are derived," how to "create their own models," and how to "think about the relationship between the models and the mathematics that is integrated" (Keck and Lott 2003, p. 131). Efforts to build coherence across the high school curriculum are of paramount importance.

Connecting and revising the curriculum

The mathematics curriculum should not only be coherent but also make connections from the mathematics curriculum to other disciplines. For example, *A Framework for K–12 Science Education* (National Research Council 2012) and the subsequently released *Next Generation Science Standards* (National Research Council 2013b) have significant importance for mathematics. The scientific and engineering practices have a great deal in common with the mathematical practices outlined in CCSSM, and indeed, "Using Mathematics and Computational Thinking" is listed as one of the science practices. Furthermore, mathematical concepts underlie much of science—for example, "Scale, proportion, and quantity" is listed as one of seven crosscutting concepts.

Finally, all curriculum-related documents (national, state or provincial, and local) need to be periodically revisited to ensure that they reflect changing priorities related to the mathematics that students need to learn, as well as new research into effective learning progressions. Although a level of stability in such documents is necessary to allow progress toward the goals that they establish, specific mechanisms should also be put in place to track changes that are needed, so that the documents can be regularly updated.

Illustration

Effective attention to curriculum involves periodic monitoring, with course revisions as needed. Consider, for example, a high school mathematics department that engages in professional development during the summer to revise a unit on congruence for the coming year. This is one of the topics that the department believes that students have not learned at the intended level in the previous two years. The teachers recognize that CCSSM includes standards for using transformations to help students make sense of congruence and that some of the approaches in the adopted textbook series do not adequately address these standards. Moreover, they know that some approaches to the topic that the book includes are not necessary to address the standards. As a result of reviewing student performance, the teachers in the department agree that they can omit two of the sections of a chapter in the book.

At one meeting, the teachers note that when the students are in middle school, they study the idea that the translation, reflection, or rotation of a figure produces a congruent shape. They also notice that an earlier chapter in the high school book involves the exploration of parabolas and how the locations of the curves, as well as their shapes, are related to their equations. They decide that rather than studying quadratic equations and parabolas early in the year and then separating this topic from congruence, they can link the content of the two chapters to make both topics more meaningful for their students.

As a group, the teachers agree to position transformations as the foundation of the unit. In the students' examination of parabolas, they will embed some review of transformations. Then, building on this theme, they will have students investigate congruence through the lens of transformational geometry. Although all this content is in the standards, they are able to reorder and restructure the material in the textbook and ancillary materials to meet the needs of the students more effectively.

When they teach the sequence of lessons that they have prepared as a team, the teachers will continually ask students to switch the lenses that they use—from looking at a situation algebraically to exploring how it connects with the geometry that they have been studying. Once they have an outline for accomplishing the goal and have made a tentative schedule for each lesson, they recognize that the next step is to identify appropriate tasks that will build the students' conceptual understanding and mathematical reasoning. They investigate tasks that are offered in the textbook as well as tasks from other curricular resources, such as websites, and they map out a restructured unit that will help students make connections and achieve at a higher level. In the coming school year, they will gather data on student success and revise the plans as needed for the future.

Moving to action

Making the Curriculum Principle a reality will require all stakeholders to focus on helping students achieve challenging standards by implementing a coherent curriculum. Teachers need to enter into dialogue with colleagues to become more familiar with the mathematical expectations of the standards that are guiding their teaching, including discussions of how these ideas are developed in both horizontal and vertical components of the curriculum. They need to evaluate the extent to which curricular materials and resources align with and support meaningful student learning of the content and practices in the standards.

Meanwhile, school administrators can support the implementation of standards by promoting meaningful professional development that assists teachers in making the most effective use of curricular materials. Administrators should recognize that pacing guides, textbooks, and other instructional materials can guide the planning process but should never take the place of the teacher in determining how to meet the needs of the students in a particular class most effectively. Finally, curriculum planners at all levels should sequence content to maximize coherence and connections across unit topics and across grade levels and courses. To accomplish this most effectively at the high school level, educators should consider an integrated approach as a way to help students understand mathematics as a discipline rather than as an isolated set of courses.

Tools and Technology

An excellent mathematics program integrates the use of mathematical tools and technology as essential resources to help students learn and make sense of mathematical ideas, reason mathematically, and communicate their mathematical thinking.

For meaningful learning of mathematics, tools and technology must be indispensable features of the classroom. Useful mathematical tools include manipulatives, such as counters, snap-cubes, base-ten blocks, pattern blocks, and building blocks in the lower grades, and algebra tiles, geoboards, protractors, compasses and straightedges, and geometric models in the upper grades. Technology includes interactive whiteboards and a wide range of handheld, tablet, laptop, and desktop-based devices that can be used to help students make sense of mathematics, engage in mathematical reasoning, and communicate mathematically.

In many schools, calculators are a commonly used technology in mathematics classrooms, ranging from those incorporating basic operations in the lower grades to more advanced graphing calculators in the upper grades. However, the technology landscape is rapidly changing. Mobile devices such as advanced smartphones and tablets using touch interfaces offer much of the functionality of desktop computers, blurring the line between advanced calculators designed specifically for mathematics and more general computing devices. Smartphones and tablets can be used to gather data, conduct classroom polls, and run applications that perform calculations, run simulations, and promote visualization by enabling students to play games that require problem-solving skills.

Thus, the platform of the technology is less important than the functionality that it provides. Computers, tablets, smartphones, and advanced calculators all make available a range of applications that support students in exploring mathematics as well as in making sense of concepts and procedures and engaging in mathematical reasoning. Graphing applications can allow students to examine multiple representations of functions and data by generating graphs, tables, and symbolic expressions that are dynamically linked. Spreadsheet applications can quickly display the results of repeated calculations and generate tables of values using a variety of graphical representations, with both of these applications allowing students to develop insights into mathematical structures and relationships. Computer algebra systems (CAS) can operate on algebraic statements. Interactive (dynamic) geometry applications allow exploration of geometric conjectures—including those in coordinate, transformational, and synthetic contexts—since dragging the objects preserves the underlying relationships among them in well-constructed diagrams. Modeling tools are useful in exploring three-dimensional objects. Data analysis applications range from more intuitive tools that are useful in the lower grades to tools that support advanced analyses and are appropriate for high school students. Many applications support dynamic representations that allow students to engage in "what if" explorations.

Moreover, having access to a range of software applications may help students explore particular mathematical situations. For example, a geoboard, whether in the form of a physical manipulative or a virtual tool like that shown in figure 23, might help students explore properties of triangles, whereas a CAS might facilitate an exploration of the parameters of functions, as shown in figure 24.

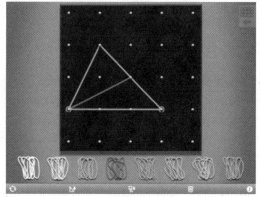

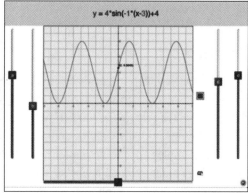

Fig. 23. A virtual model of a geoboard on a tablet device

Fig. 24. Use of an app to explore the effects of the parameters in the sine function

The use of electronic tools often focuses on what Dick and Hollebrands (2011) call "mathematical action technologies," which produce mathematical responses based on user input, allowing students to explore mathematical ideas and observe, make, and test conjectures about mathematical relationships. Note that mathematical action is also embedded in the use of non-electronic mathematical tools, such as physical manipulatives.

Nonmathematical technologies and tools (e.g., word processing, presentation software, and communications applications) can also support interactions in the mathematics classroom (Cohen and Hollebrands 2011). For example, student responses to an interactive poll can be quickly gathered through the use of either a dedicated clicker system or applications on a range of mobile device platforms, to provide teachers with formative information that may help guide instruction. Interactive whiteboards, document cameras, and Web-based presentation applications can help students communicate their thinking to classmates and receive constructive feedback. Students' sharing of work can occur beyond the boundaries of the face-to-face classroom through the use of secure Web-based platforms to post and comment on student-made podcasts, digital images of student work, and student presentation files. Students might use text messaging, cloud-based shared documents, virtual whiteboards, blogs, or wikis to collaborate on mathematics problems within a school or with students in other states or provinces or even countries (Roschelle et al. 2010). By making use of these electronic tools, students have a greater sense of ownership of the mathematics that they are learning, since the applications promote a sense of shared enterprise in the learning of mathematics.

Finally, a wide variety of Web-based resources support the teaching and learning of mathematics. Teachers are increasingly using personal and shared pages to organize and categorize the resources that they find most useful. These lists allow them to quickly locate resources that they have found useful in the past and share these with others through social media. Their capacity to do this represents, in a sense, the virtual opening of the classroom door to allow for collaboration among classrooms and teachers. Furthermore, teachers can organize shared pages to enhance communication with their students and their students' parents or caregivers.

Obstacles

Many schools and teachers pride themselves on being up-to-date with the latest technology and tools. However, the value of the technology depends on whether students actually engage with specific technologies or tools in ways that promote mathematical reasoning and sense making. Having students watch a computer presentation or tutorial in which mathematical facts and examples appear, no matter how visually engaging, is not significantly different from having students watch a teacher write the same information on an interactive whiteboard or chalkboard, and thus it is no more effective in giving students access to or making sense of mathematical ideas. Having students watch an online lecture does no more to promote the mathematical practices than watching a live lecture. In the name of "flipping" a classroom, some teachers require students to view a Web-based lecture in the evening and then complete worksheets in class, but this arrangement may do no more to engage students in making sense of mathematics than lecturing in class and having students fill out worksheets for homework. The key issue is whether students in the flipped classroom are engaged in active learning, solving problems that promote reasoning and build understanding. At the present time, no consistent scientific research evidence suggests that flipping, in the absence of an increased focus on conceptual learning and student sense making, is an instructional practice that improves student learning (Goodwin and Miller 2013). Mathematics teachers should judiciously adopt technology that supports effective instruction but not simply for the sake of using more technology in the classroom.

Likewise, teachers may merely teach students procedures for using tools or technology to solve problems without giving them opportunities to think through the problems or to connect the procedures with more formal mathematical reasoning. For example, a teacher may give students steps to use base-ten blocks to solve multi-digit addition problems without offering them opportunities to use the blocks to explore the mathematical meaning behind algorithms for multi-digit addition. Further, although applications designed to drill students on mathematical facts and procedures can develop recall and fluency if students have already developed understanding of a topic, using such applications will not produce conceptual understanding (Erlwanger 2004).

Schools, parents, and teachers sometimes limit students' use of mathematical tools and technology for fear that they will become a crutch. To guard against this result, they allow students to use tools and technology only to check answers or as a reward after learning to solve the problems by using paper and pencil. In the elementary grades, teachers may believe that use of calculators will prevent students from mastering basic number combinations. In the upper grades, teachers may think that use of technology will prevent students from developing the level of algebraic skill that they need for further study. In some cases, only gifted or high-achieving students are given opportunities to use tools to explore advanced topics while other students are relegated to using technology in ways that focus on lower-level skills. In such instances, physical or virtual manipulatives may be used in the primary grades only to provide a "fun activity" or a diversion from the normal routine; in later grades, such tools are sometimes seen as juvenile and unnecessary. When situations like these occur, opportunities for maximizing the potential of mathematical tools and technology to support and enhance mathematical learning are missed.

Furthermore, instruction sometimes incorporates mathematical technology in ways that do not promote mathematical reasoning, sense making, or communication. Teachers may incorporate technology merely as a computational aid that students use without regard to its limitations or thought about the results that it provides. Thus, when students (or teachers) use calculators or spreadsheets to find answers, they may accept the displayed results as the correct answers without considering whether these results make sense or how they apply to the context of the problem. Moreover, students may reflexively apply a favored tool (physical or virtual) without thinking about, or having a teacher challenge them to think about, its appropriateness or whether another approach might be more fruitful. These unproductive uses of tools and technology limit students' opportunities to reason with and about mathematics and demonstrate the importance of the role of teachers who have a deep knowledge of mathematics and understand how such tools and technology can be used strategically in ways that support meaningful learning.

A number of obstacles outside the classroom also have an impact on the effective use of tools and technology. In some schools, particularly schools of poverty, technology and other tools may not be available as a result of inequitable distribution of resources. Moreover, teachers may not have access to technology or adequate training in its effective use to promote students' mathematical learning. In some cases, potentially valuable technology and tools may sit unused in closets or on shelves, or they may be used in unproductive ways. Some schools are well equipped with Internet-ready computers but have outdated wireless connections that provide inconsistent access to Web-based tools. Also, textbooks and curricular materials may claim to incorporate tools and technology but fail to do so in ways that help teachers promote reasoning and sense making, thus increasing teachers' difficulty in finding appropriate activities. In some textbooks, the use of technology is set off in a box or presented as an added-on feature, as if to suggest that the approach is optional and unnecessary. Finally, state or provincial policies may drastically limit the use of tools and technology in required assessments, and as a result, teachers may be reluctant to allow students to use technology that will not be available to them on the assessments.

The following table compares some unproductive and productive beliefs that influence the implementation of classroom tools and technology. It is important to note that these beliefs should not be viewed as good or bad, but rather as productive when they support effective teaching and learning or unproductive when they limit student access to important mathematics content and practices.

Beliefs about tools and technology in learning mathematics	
Unproductive beliefs	Productive beliefs
Calculators and other tools are at best a frill or distraction and at worst a crutch that keeps students from learning mathematics. Students should use these tools only after they have learned how to do procedures with paper and pencil.	Technology is an inescapable fact of life in the world in which we live and should be embraced as a powerful tool for doing mathematics. Using technology can assist students in visualizing and understanding important mathematical concepts and support students' mathematical reasoning and problem solving.
School mathematics is static. What students need to know about mathematics is unchanged (or maybe even threatened) by the presence of technology.	Technology and other tools not only change how to teach but also affect what can be taught. They can assist students in investigating mathematical ideas and problems that might otherwise be too difficult or time-consuming to explore.
Physical and virtual manipulatives should be used only with very young children who need visuals and opportunities to explore by moving objects.	Students at all grade levels can benefit from the use of physical and virtual manipulative materials to provide visual models of a range of mathematical ideas.
Technology should be used primarily as a quick way to get correct answers to computations.	Finding answers to a mathematical computation is not sufficient. Students need to understand whether an answer is reasonable and how the results apply to a given context. They also need to be able to consider the relative usefulness of a range of tools in particular contexts.
Only select individuals, such as the most advanced students or students who reside in districts that choose technology as a budgetary priority, should have access to technology and tools, since these are optional supplements to mathematics learning.	All students should have access to technology and other tools that support the teaching and learning of mathematics.
Using technology and other tools to teach is easy. Just launch the app or website, or hand out the manipulatives, and let the students work on their own.	Effective use of technology and other tools requires careful planning. Teachers need appropriate professional development to learn how to use them effectively.

Beliefs about tools and technology in learning mathematics, *continued*	
Unproductive beliefs	**Productive beliefs**
Online instructional videos can replace classroom instruction.	Online instructional videos must be judiciously adopted and used to support, not replace, effective instruction.

Overcoming the obstacles

Physical and virtual manipulatives, as well as other concrete models, can help students visualize mathematical relationships (Roschelle et al. 2010). Research suggests that about two-thirds of high school juniors and seniors are still functioning at a concrete level of thinking (Orlich 2000). Consequently, manipulatives can play an important role for a wide range of students—from helping younger students visualize multi-digit multiplication by using base-ten blocks to allowing older students to make sense of completing the square by using algebra tiles.

Mathematical tools and technology can be useful as students work on solving challenging mathematical problems and can enhance students' communication about mathematics to others.

Use of tools and technology for all students

Technology is an inherent part of students' lives. Many students use smartphones to interact constantly with their peers through social media, and they expect to have instant access to the information that they need. Technology is an integral part of nearly all careers that they may choose to pursue as adults. Mathematics classrooms must reflect this reality, incorporating technology as an integral part of instruction.

Despite popular belief, use of technology does not inhibit students' learning of mathematics. The idea that it does is particularly prevalent regarding the use of calculators. However, after conducting a comprehensive literature review, Ronau and others (2011, p. 1) concluded the following:

> In general, we found that the body of research consistently shows that the use of calculators in the teaching and learning of mathematics does not contribute to any negative outcomes for skill development or procedural proficiency, but instead enhances the understanding of mathematics concepts and student orientation toward mathematics.

As NCTM (2011) asserts in a position statement, students should have "regular access to technologies that support and advance mathematical sense making, reasoning, problem solving, and communication." However, denying or limiting student access to technology at particular times to achieve goals related to fluency may be appropriate and even necessary.

Mathematical action technologies

"Mathematical action technologies" (Dick and Hollebrands 2011) provide opportunities for students to interact with mathematical ideas. Thus, students may interact with an on-screen representation of a manipulative to explore mathematical relationships. They may use a program to create representations of a large data set to explore relationships and draw conclusions. Or they may carry out a set of related computations that would be time-consuming to do by hand to look for patterns in the results. The ability to shift between different representations of a problem (e.g., visual/graphical, symbolic, numerical) can help students develop a deeper understanding of mathematical concepts. Further, research suggests that the effect of working with virtual manipulatives on a computer screen is equivalent to using physical materials (Sarama and Clements 2009). Multi-touch interfaces may also make interactions with computer representations more natural for younger students and older students alike.

However, teachers need to recognize how taking full advantage of the power of tools and technology can effectively enhance learning. They need to help students connect their observations from exploration with understanding of the mathematics behind the situation. Students and teachers need to understand both the power and limitations of tools and technology, acknowledging the need to ensure that answers are considered both for their reasonableness and for their applicability to the context in which the manipulation or computation took place. In the end, tools and technology are only a means, not an end; they cannot supplant student understanding and reasonable levels of computational fluency (NCTM 2000).

Teachers need to recognize that mathematical action technology influences not only *how* they teach but also *what* they are able to teach. For example, a graphing application on a mobile device can be used to explore the graphs of a series of linear functions, such as $y = 2x - 5$, $y = 2x + 1$, and $y = 2x + 7$. Students can be asked to determine what the lines have in common, how they are different, and how changing specific values in the equations affect the graphs. By using an interactive slider, students can change the coefficients and constants and immediately see the effects of the changes on the graphs. In doing so, students can reason that the coefficient of the x-value determines the slope (making the lines parallel when the coefficients are equivalent across the functions), while the constant determines the y-intercept. The teacher can then build on this conclusion by challenging students to graph a set of linear functions on paper without the use of a value table. Thus, instead of having students begin with pencil and paper and leaving work with technology until after the mastery of the skill, the teacher can use the graphing application to develop the students' conceptual understanding of the effects of changing parameters of linear functions. Traditional paper-and-pencil methods of drawing graphs need not precede the use of technology.

Policies and professional development

Without well-designed professional development, teachers may feel uncomfortable about using tools and technology in their classrooms. However, once they understand the role of tools and technology as a support for student reasoning and sense making, teachers come to see that they allow opportunities to pose more challenging questions that focus on exploration and understanding.

Meaningful professional development that focuses on mathematics-specific uses of tools and technology is essential to their effective use in the classroom. Providing generic workshops on interactive whiteboards or presentation software may not help teachers make the necessary connections of tools and technology to the Mathematics Teaching Practices. They need to develop deep understandings of how technology and tools can be used to investigate mathematical ideas, generate multiple representations of a mathematical construct, and solve mathematics problems. They need to reflect on how their students might use these tools and how the tools might be incorporated into the curriculum in a meaningful way.

Effective professional development should also focus on enhancing teachers' abilities to use technology to collaborate with colleagues locally and globally as well as to communicate with parents and caregivers. Moreover, teachers need to explore innovative ways in which they can have students use technology to describe their mathematical thinking and collaborate with classmates. Given the accelerating pace of technological innovation, teachers need to continually seek out ways in which technology can support students' learning of mathematics.

Policies and practices must support the effective use of mathematical tools and technology throughout the mathematics program. Appropriate use of such tools should be incorporated into state or provincial and local standards and curricular frameworks, and assessments should not only allow but also require the use of technology. Selection of textbooks and instructional materials should include consideration of whether these resources incorporate mathematical tools and technology in ways that support students' proficiency in the mathematical practices and teachers' implementation of the Mathematical Teaching Practices.

Illustration

Figure 25 shows how Ms. Lorenzo, an eighth-grade teacher, engages her students in a real-world context related to baseball while making effective classroom use of a variety of tools and technology to develop their understanding and skill in writing equations and solving systems of equations. By using color counters, laptop computers, graphing calculators, electronic tablets, and a document reader to display their strategies, students are able to enter into the problem in a variety of ways and find the solution by using the tools that make the most sense to them.

An eighth-grade teacher, Ms. Lorenzo, has her students work on the concepts of writing equations and finding the solution to a system of equations by exploring a problem involving baseball, since the Little League World Series is currently on television. The problem lends itself to exploration with a variety of mathematical tools, both physical and technological:

> At a baseball game in April, a batter came to the plate, and the scoreboard showed that he had a batting average of .132. After two pitches, he hit a single into center field, and the scoreboard immediately updated his average to .154. Given this information, determine how many at-bats he has had so far this season, and how many hits he has had.

Seated in groups, students begin exploring the problem. To visualize it, a student in one group picks up a set of two-color counters from the table and lays down two of them—one red and one yellow—and says, "Red stands for a hit. If the player bats twice, and one chip is red, he has a batting average of 1/2, or 0.5." He places another red counter on the table, noting that the batter has now increased his average from 0.5 to 0.667, "since two out of three counters are now red." He continues to add red counters, comparing the resulting numbers of red to the total numbers of counters on the table.

Students throughout the classroom continue to guess-and-check to narrow their choices and arrive at a solution. But one group decides that using a spreadsheet on a laptop computer might speed things up, letting them keep track of their guesses easily. They "fill down" their formula, as shown below in (a), looking at differences between rows. With some guidance from their teacher, they decide that they need a different kind of electronic spreadsheet table, as shown in (b). This table computes the number of hits for a given number of at-bats, and then it computes the average for one more hit in one more at-bat. Noting that their data for 40 at-bats (with 5.28 hits) shows a percentage that is close to 0.132, they try numbers of at-bats close to 40. A student remarks, "It looks like 38 or 39 is really close, but we're not sure how to decide which it is."

	A	B	C
1	Hits	Total	Average
2	5	38	0.132
3	6	39	0.15384615
4	7	40	0.175
5	8	41	0.19512195
6	9	42	0.21428571
7	10	43	0.23255814

(a)

	A	B	C	D	E	F
1	Hits	Total	Average	Hits+1	Total+1	Average
2	1.32	10	0.132	2.32	11	0.21090909
3	2.64	20	0.132	3.64	21	0.17333333
4	3.96	30	0.132	4.96	31	0.16
5	5.28	40	0.132	6.28	41	0.15317073
6	6.6	50	0.132	7.6	51	0.14901961
7	7.92	60	0.132	8.92	61	0.14622951

(b)

Fig. 25. An eighth-grade teacher's use of technology to develop mathematical skill and understanding

In another group, students who are using a guess-and-check approach notice a repeating pattern in their calculations: each time, they begin with a number of hits and at-bats, find the batting average, add 1 to both the hits and at-bats, and then calculate the new average. One of the students suggests trying to use an algebraic approach to the problem. The group agrees on the following solution, as later explained by one team member to the class:

If x represents the number of times the player has batted, and y stands for the number of hits, then $\frac{y}{x}$ would determine the batting average. So, when the player bats and gets a hit, his new average could be represented as

$$\frac{y+1}{x+1}.$$

That allowed us to write two different equations—one representing the original batting average and the other his average after he gets a hit in his next at-bat:

$$\frac{y}{x} = 0.132 \text{ and } \frac{y+1}{x+1} = 0.154$$

We decided we could find the solution if we used a graphing app on our tablet to see where the two equations intersect. But first we had to solve them for y to enter them. Here is the graph we got [see (c)]. We also thought the answer should be around 38 or 39. When we zoomed in, we decided that 38 is closer.

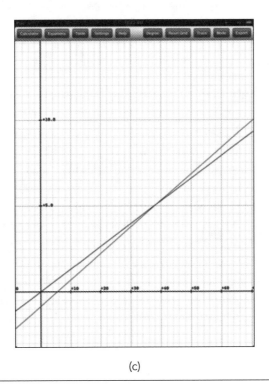

(c)

Fig. 25. *Continued*

Another group took a similar approach but used the table function on a graphing calculator, and a student from this group notes, "We agree that 38 looks like the best answer for the number of at-bats. But we're confused because our table doesn't show the exact answer—how can you have 5.016 hits?"

Ms. Lorenzo then leads a discussion on rounding and precision and checks to be sure that the students can interpret the meaning of x, $x + 1$, y, and $y + 1$ in the context of the problem. She also poses a question: "Did anyone do this without using a calculator or tablet? Take a minute to see how you might approach the problem."

Most groups agree that substitution would probably be easiest, although some groups substituted $0.132x$ for y in the equation

$$\frac{y+1}{x+1} = 0.154,$$

while others simply equated the two expressions that they found when solving for y to enter them into their calculator or computer.

Finally, one student asks, "Could there be a different answer for this question? Isn't it possible that the person was 10 for 76 instead of 5 for 38? Since $10/76$ is equivalent to $5/38$, we really can't know how many times he was at bat." Other students quickly reject this possibility, since $11/75$ is not equal to 0.154. And another student remarks, "In the graph, we had two lines, and we know that they can intersect at only one point."

Fig. 25. *Continued*

Moving to action

The rapid pace at which technology is evolving necessitates ongoing reexamination of the priorities of effective mathematics programs. Students are growing up with advanced technologies—from mobile devices to Web-based applications—and it is essential that teachers receive the professional development necessary to keep up with the changes. Teachers should continually explore mathematical tools and technologies to evaluate their potential to open students' mathematical horizons and to look for ways in which technology may change how students use mathematics in college and careers. Given the accelerating ease with which technology can be used to carry out nearly any mathematical procedure that students might be asked to perform, mathematics educators may need to raise questions about the balance of procedural and conceptual knowledge required for mathematical proficiency. Administrators and policymakers need to continue to emphasize the importance of developing meaningful learning of mathematics while recognizing that effective mathematics programs reflect the evolving power of tools and technology to transform how mathematics is used to solve real-world problems.

Assessment

An excellent mathematics program ensures that assessment is an integral part of instruction, provides evidence of proficiency with important mathematics content and practices, includes a variety of strategies and data sources, and informs feedback to students, instructional decisions, and program improvement.

When asked for a definition of *assessment*, many educators think of quizzes and tests, as well as district, state or provincial, and national measures of student achievement. However, assessment needs to be viewed much more broadly. In *Assessment Standards for School Mathematics* (1995), NCTM defined assessment as "the process of gathering evidence about a student's knowledge of, ability to use, and disposition toward, mathematics and of making inferences from that evidence for a variety of purposes" (p. 3). At the same time, NCTM posited that assessment should serve four distinct functions in school mathematics:

- *Monitoring students' progress* to promote student learning

- *Making instructional decisions* to modify instruction to facilitate student learning

- *Evaluating students' achievement* to summarize and report students' demonstrated understanding at a particular moment in time

- *Evaluating programs* to make decisions about instructional programs

Furthermore, in *Principles and Standards for School Mathematics* (2000), NCTM asserted that assessment should "support the learning of important mathematics and furnish useful information to both teachers and students" (p. 22). According to Wiliam (2011, p. 43), "An assessment functions formatively to the extent that evidence about student achievement is elicited, interpreted, and used by teachers, learners, or their peers to make decisions about the next steps in instruction that are likely to be better than the decisions they would have made in the absence of that evidence." Assessment, then, in the context of effective mathematics instruction, is a process whose primary purpose is to gather data that support the teaching and learning of mathematics.

Obstacles

Although assessment should support student learning, too often it functions in schools as an obstacle to promoting mathematics success for all students. The reason for this is that assessment traditionally tends to emphasize the evaluation of student achievement (e.g., the assignment of grades), and more recently, the rating of schools and the performance of teachers. This cultural perception that links assessment to grading and rating has dominated thinking in North America since the beginning of schooling, but it has become more pronounced in the last decade as schools and systems have increasingly used high-stakes assessments to evaluate the effectiveness of teachers, schools, and administrators. One consequence of the focus on assessment for accountability has been the unnecessary politicization of assessment. In the name of accountability, the rich potential for using assessment processes to strengthen student learning and improve instruction has been diminished.

Assessment is often viewed and practiced as a periodic externally imposed event (e.g., annual state or provincial testing; quarterly district tests) or as an individual teacher-conducted activity that interrupts instruction—both of which treat assessment as something that is "done to" students. Externally created summative assessments are frequently little more than multiple-choice surveys of a broad set of low-level procedural skills that do not assess students' mathematical understanding and problem-solving abilities (Herman and Linn 2013). Consequently, the results of external assessment frequently fail to provide teachers and students with the descriptive, accurate, and timely feedback that teachers need to improve instruction and advance learning (Reeves 2011).

Moreover, important judgments about students, such as placement in courses, and about teachers, such as future employment or performance-based pay, too often are significantly influenced by the results of a single high-stakes test. This decision making ignores the variability that may occur as a result of multiple factors affecting student performance on high-stakes tests. One major factor can be the design of the test itself. A fundamental psychometric principle of test design is discrimination—that is, "good" test items are those that produce differences in performance (Haladyna and Downing 1989). In the name of discrimination, tests may contain items that underestimate students' actual knowledge. For example, consider the item in figure 26.

At the school carnival, Carmen sold 3 times as many hot dogs as Shawn. The two of them sold 152 hot dogs altogether. How many hot dogs did Carmen sell?

(a) 21   (b) 38   (c) 51   (d) 114   (e) 148

Fig. 26. An algebra standardized test item

The most common answer given by students is (b), which is the intermediate result—the number of hot dogs that Shawn sold—instead of the correct answer of (d), the number of hot dogs that Carmen sold. Unfortunately, even though students who answer (b) correctly perform most of the procedures that the task requires, this understanding is not reflected in their scores.

Results of standardized and classroom assessments (teacher created or publisher provided) are not always analyzed appropriately and used to improve instruction. When a school district simply enters standardized test scores in its database rather than supporting teachers through formal structures to discuss the implications of measured strengths and weaknesses of the mathematics program, a significant learning opportunity is missed.

Alternatively, standardized test results can be overanalyzed and misinterpreted. For example, teachers and administrators often focus on simple increases and decreases in test scores, ignoring whether such changes are statistically significant. Moreover, educators tend to make assumptions about students' knowledge without considering specific test items and the validity of the information that these items provide about that knowledge. For example, one such assumption is that students who answered the hot dog item incorrectly lacked any understanding of the underlying mathematics.

Finally, some teachers view assessment as analogous to grading and may not recognize the value of collecting data about students' thinking and understanding—data that may not translate easily into an elementary report card mark or a secondary course grade. Although traditional tests and quizzes can shed light on student progress, other rich sources of information—from sample interviews to observations, daily exit slips, and journal writing—can also inform teachers of students' understanding and suggest instructional modifications. Thinking of assessment as limited to "testing" student learning rather than as a process that can advance it has been an obstacle to the effective use of assessment processes for decades.

The following table compares some unproductive and productive beliefs that influence assessment practices. It is important to note that these beliefs should not be viewed as good or bad, but rather as productive when they support effective teaching and learning or unproductive when they limit student access to important mathematics content and practices.

Beliefs about mathematics assessment	
Unproductive beliefs	**Productive beliefs**
The primary purpose of assessment is accountability for students through report card marks or grades.	The primary purpose of assessment is to inform and improve the teaching and learning of mathematics.
Assessment in the classroom is an interruption of the instructional process.	Assessment is an ongoing process that is embedded in instruction to support student learning and make adjustments to instruction.
Only multiple-choice and other "objective" paper-and-pencil tests can measure mathematical knowledge reliably and accurately.	Mathematical understanding and processes can be measured through the use of a variety of assessment strategies and tasks.
A single assessment can be used to make important decisions about students and teachers.	Multiple data sources are needed to provide an accurate picture of teacher and student performance.

Beliefs about mathematics assessment, *continued*	
Unproductive beliefs	**Productive beliefs**
Assessment is something that is done *to* students.	Assessment is a process that should help students become better judges of their own work, assist them in recognizing high-quality work when they produce it, and support them in using evidence to advance their own learning.
Stopping teaching to review and take practice tests improves students' performance on high-stakes tests.	Ongoing review and distributed practice within effective instruction are productive test preparation strategies.

Overcoming the obstacles

Effective assessment supports and enhances the learning of important mathematics by furnishing useful formative and summative information to both teachers and students. Effective assessment of mathematics learning is a process that is coherently aligned with learning goals, makes deliberate use of the data gathered as evidence of learning, and provides guidance for next instructional steps and programmatic decision making. In excellent mathematics programs, students learn to assess and recognize high quality in their own work.

Assessing conceptual understanding, reasoning, and procedural fluency

Effective classroom and external assessment provides evidence about all components of students' mathematics learning. The evidence obtained depends on the questions and tasks used. More specifically, obtaining evidence about understanding and reasoning requires the use of tasks and methods designed for those purposes. For example, to assess students' understanding of a concept, one might ask students to explain it to someone else, represent the concept in multiple ways, apply their knowledge of skills to solve simple and complex problems, reverse givens and unknowns in a problem situation, or compare and contrast a mathematical concept with other concepts (National Center on Education and the Economy and the University of Pittsburgh 1997).

Consider the TV Sales task shown in figure 27. Part A provides evidence about students' ability to make sense of a problem situation and apply procedural skills in working with percentages to determine a solution. Part B asks students to evaluate whether the reasoning in two different approaches is equivalent and to explain their thinking.

Grade 7: TV Sales

A store is advertising a sale with 10% off all items in the store. Sales tax is 5%.

Part A

A 32-inch television is regularly priced at $295.00. What is the total price of the television, including sales tax, if it was purchased on sale? Fill in the blank to complete the sentence. Round your answer to the nearest cent.

The total cost of the television is $_____.

Part B

Adam and Brandi are customers discussing how the discount and tax will be calculated.

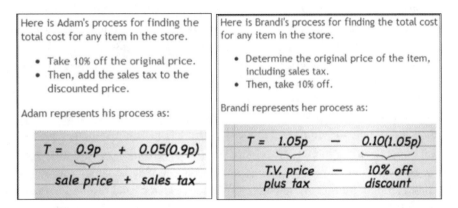

In both equations, *T* represents the total cost of the television and *p* represents the regular price.

Are they both correct? Use the properties of operations to justify your answer.

Fig. 27. TV Sales task. From PARCC (2013).

Short questions or writing prompts such as the following can be used to assess students' conceptual understanding and reasoning:

- Create a situation that could be modeled with $6 \div 3/4$.

- Write three equations, one with no solution, one with exactly one solution, and one with infinitely many solutions.

- Is $12 \div 3$ the same as $3 \div 12$? Explain.

Teachers can assign these writing prompts prior to introducing a new mathematics topic to determine students' background knowledge. In turn, the assessment data may influence the design of the entire sequence of lessons in the unit. A key question for teachers to consider in creating or selecting assessment tasks and items is, What evidence will this provide about students' mathematical knowledge?

Leveraging formative assessment results

Depending on how the results of assessment are used, assessments in mathematics can be organized into two categories—formative and summative. To achieve the threefold purpose of motivating, supporting, and improving student learning and instruction, teachers can view and practice assessment at the classroom level primarily as a formative process—an ongoing and continual real-time collection of data as students participate in mathematics instruction in the classroom. Teachers continually monitor and respond to their students' progress through formal and informal means, including—but not limited to—effective questioning and classroom discussion, conducting interviews with individual students, having students respond to prompts in math journals, answering real-time questions through the use of clickers or mobile devices, or responding to a prompt on an exit slip. In this work, teachers *elicit and use evidence of student thinking* as the Mathematics Teaching Practices recommend. The earlier discussion of this practice provides additional guidance on implementing ongoing formative assessment processes during instruction.

Research indicates that making formative assessment processes an integral component of instruction is associated with improved student learning (Black and Wiliam 1998b; Hattie, 2009, 2012; Popham 2008). In fact, the research on the effectiveness of formative assessment processes to advance student learning met the National Mathematics Advisory Panel's (NMAP 2008) strict definition of "scientifically based research" and resulted in the panel's finding that "teachers' regular use of formative assessment improves their students' learning" and its recommendation that teachers make "regular use of formative assessment " to improve mathematics achievement (p. xxiii).

What ultimately distinguishes assessment processes as summative or formative is how the results of assessment are used. The defining characteristic of formative assessment "is that evidence about student learning is used to adjust instruction to better meet student needs" (Wiliam 2007b, p. 191). Under this definition, even traditional classroom assessments that are typically used only in summative ways—including publisher- or teacher-created chapter or unit tests, which are used primarily to assign students grades—can be formatively repurposed to modify and guide instruction to meet students' learning needs.

When viewed as a process that is indistinguishable from effective instruction, assessment serves as a means to achieve productive teaching and learning for all, rather than merely as the final stage in the traditional teach-learn-assess cycle. Moreover, when teachers place greater emphasis on formative assessment processes, their use of instructional time may become more effective (NMAP 2008), and this in turn may lead to a reduction in the time that they spend preparing their students for state, provincial, or national assessments. Using effective teaching practices and achieving success on accountability assessments do not have to be perceived as mutually exclusive (Martin et al. 2011).

In fact, research indicates that standardized test scores are lower in schools where teachers spend large amounts of time engaged in "test prep" activities—practicing test questions while putting regular instruction on hold—compared with schools where teachers continue regular instruction (e.g., Allensworth, Correa, and Ponisciak 2008). Providing students with periodic opportunities to practice using concepts and skills, along with feedback about their performance, helps students solidify their knowledge and promotes retention, reflection, generalization, and transfer of knowledge and skill (Pashler et al. 2007). In short, effective instruction, including formative assessment, is arguably the most effective test-preparation strategy.

A focus on students

At the center of the assessment process is the student. An important goal of assessment should be to make students effective self-assessors, teaching them how to recognize the strengths and weaknesses of past performance and use them to to improve their future work. Students should be provided with examples of high-quality work and then be given feedback that they can act on to advance their own learning and help them attain their goals. Peer assessments can usefully allow students to compare their work critically with that of class-mates. Eventually, students should be able to recognize high-quality work when they produce it. When students assume assessment responsibilities in these ways, teachers and students work as partners in the learning process, with teachers and other students giving advice on how to improve (Stiggins 2007).

This vision of assessment is very different from the traditional image of assessments that are administered at the end of a unit, primarily to determine grades. Assessment obviously and appropriately has a role in the assignment of report card marks or course grades. However, an exclusive emphasis on end-of-unit assessments, shutting out formative assessment processes and making no use of their power to advance student learning, carries a serious risk. This narrow use of assessment serves only to sort students and to convince many who earn lower grades that they cannot do mathematics, thus defeating the overall aim of ensuring mathe-matical success for all students.

Illustration

Effective formative assessment involves using tasks that elicit evidence of students' learning, then using that evidence to inform subsequent instruction. In the illustration that follows, a collaborative team of third-grade teachers modified routine end-of-unit assessment items to provide detailed information about students' understanding of multi-digit addition and subtraction and then used that information in instructional planning:

> Whitney Elementary School has a well-established professional learning community culture. Teachers work in grade-level collaborative teams to create common unit assessments, analyze students' performance, and determine instructional implications, including interventions, which they also plan together.

> The three teachers on the third-grade team met to analyze students' performance on an end-of-unit assessment on multi-digit computation. The unit supported students in making progress toward the following CCSSM content standard: "Fluently add and subtract within 1000 using strategies and algorithms based on place value, properties of operations, and/or the relationship between addition and subtraction" (CCSSM 3.NBT.2; NGO Center and CCSSO 2010, p. 24).

> This year, the team decided to use an assessment that provided information about students' strategies and reasoning in solving two subtraction problems, $823 - 365$ and $408 - 217$. The previous year's test contained ten addition and ten subtraction problems, and student proficiency was defined as a percentage of correct answers. This year's adoption of new standards prompted the teachers to gather evidence of understanding and insight into students' strategies. Thus, they asked the students to solve each problem in two different ways, provide a written explanation of their solution strategies, and use addition to show that their answers were correct. The team included checking with addition to obtain evidence from students' work on the two subtraction problems of their understanding of multi-digit addition as well as multi-digit subtraction. Figure 28 shows a student's response to one of these problems.

> The teachers sorted students' responses on the basis of the strategies used and understanding demonstrated. Overall, they were pleased with the results, noting that most students were able to produce at least one reliable and meaningful strategy for both addition and subtraction. To provide additional support for students who were still struggling, the teachers assigned these students to one of three intervention groups according to the level of place-value understanding that they showed in their strategies. Each teacher would work with one intervention group during the first twenty minutes of their ninety-minute mathematics block; then the students would return to their regular mathematics class for the day's lesson. Students not needing intervention had other assignments for this time.

Solve 408 – 217 using two different strategies. Provide an explanation of both of your strategies. Then check your answer using addition.

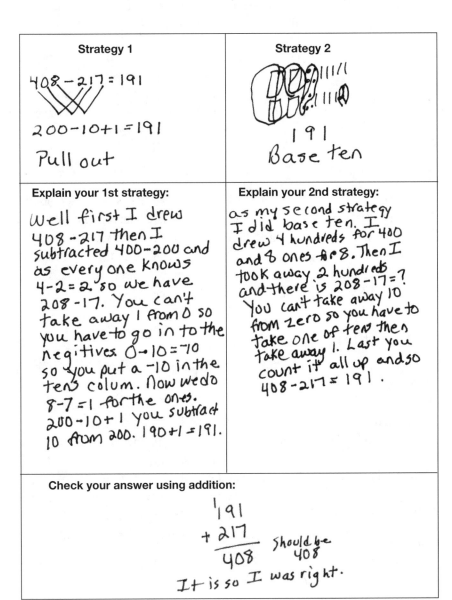

Strategy 1	Strategy 2

Strategy 1:

$408 - 217 = 191$

$200 - 10 + 1 = 191$

Pull out

Strategy 2:

191

Base ten

Explain your 1st strategy:

Well first I drew 408 – 217 then I subtracted 400 – 200 and as every one knows 4 – 2 = 2 so we have 208 – 17. You can't take away 1 from 0 so you have to go in to the negitives 0 – 10 = ⁻10 so you put a ⁻10 in the tens colum. Now we do 8 – 7 = 1 for the ones. 200 – 10 + 1 you subtract 10 from 200. 190 + 1 = 191.

Explain your 2nd strategy:

as my second strategy I did base ten. I drew 4 hundreds for 400 and 8 ones for 8. Then I took away 2 hundreds and there is 208 – 17 = ? You can't take away 10 from zero so you have to take one of tens then take away 1. Last you count it all up and so 408 – 217 = 191.

Check your answer using addition:

$$\begin{array}{r} {}^1 191 \\ + 217 \\ \hline 408 \end{array}$$

Should be 408

It is so I was right.

Fig. 28. A third-grade student's work on an end-of-unit assessment item

Finally, the teachers noted the high number of students who had made careless errors on this assessment. Although the teachers pointed these out to students in class and encouraged them to check their work and correct their mistakes, they were concerned that students would continue to make such errors on the district's quarterly benchmark assessment, resulting in an underestimation of the number of students considered to be "proficient" in multi-digit addition and subtraction.

After some conversation, the teachers realized that although they had all been saying, "Check your work," they had not actually taught their students *how* to check their work (e.g., checking to see that the numbers that they used in their computation were the same as those given in the problem). To address this situation, the teachers jointly planned a "How to Check Your Work" activity, and they decided that it would incorporate students' suggestions about how to check work. The outcome would be a "Check Your Work" routine to help students perform this task regularly.

As the illustration shows, a few well-designed tasks can provide as much or more information about students' learning as a test with many items. Also, interventions that address students' needs can be more effective when grade-level or course teachers share responsibility for interventions of all students. Finally, analysis of assessment results can reveal important aspects of learning that instruction has not addressed, or even targeted, such as the need to check one's work with full understanding of what that process involves.

Moving to action

Shifting the primary focus and function of assessment from accountability to effective instructional practice is an essential component of ensuring mathematical success for all students. Classroom teachers and school and district leaders can immediately begin to implement more effective assessment practices to reposition assessment as a formative process. Policymakers can work to ensure that assessment systems provide evidence about students' proficiency in the full range of expected mathematics outcomes—mathematical practices and conceptual understanding, as well as procedural fluency—and consider how to use the results of student achievement more appropriately. Moreover, leveraging assessment as a strategy to improve instruction and student learning at the classroom and school level is a highly cost-effective instructional strategy in comparison with other instructional improvement efforts.

Professionalism

In an excellent mathematics program, educators hold themselves and their colleagues accountable for the mathematical success of every student and for personal and collective professional growth toward effective teaching and learning of mathematics.

A professional does not accept the status quo, even when it is reasonably good, and continually seeks to learn and grow (Collins 2001). A professional upholds standards of the profession, both individually and through peer review; is focused on student learning; knows and implements the research-informed practices of the field; and uses accumulated insights and experiences to seek, both individually and collectively, improvements in existing conditions and outcomes (Wiggins and McTighe 1998).

In education, professionals who are responsible for students' mathematics learning are never satisfied with their accomplishments and are always working to increase the impact that they have on their students' mathematics learning. They aim for career-long professional growth for this reason. As professionals, mathematics teachers recognize that their own learning is never finished and continually seek to improve and enhance their mathematical knowledge for teaching, their knowledge of mathematical pedagogy, and their knowledge of students as learners of mathematics.

Mathematics teachers are professionals who do not do this work in isolation. They cultivate and support a culture of professional collaboration and continual improvement, driven by an abiding sense of interdependence and collective responsibility. Schools that support success for all students are characterized by a collective sense of responsibility for improvement (Williams 2003) and a sense of collective efficacy—a belief that the instructional staff has the capacity to implement the actions necessary to make a difference for their students (Barber and Mourshed 2007; Hoy, Tarter, and Hoy 2006). Mathematics educators must hold themselves, individually and collectively, accountable for *all* students' learning, not just the learning of their own students. Within a culture of professionalism, educators embrace the transparency of their work, their accomplishments, and their challenges, and they share ideas, insights, and practices as they collaborate in ways that build on individual strengths and overcome individual challenges to ensure mathematical success for all students. Furthermore, this collaboration can be enhanced through the efforts of math coaches or specialists who serve as mentors to assist and coordinate mathematics teaching in a classroom, school, or district.

Teachers of mathematics also recognize that they are engaged in a mathematical profession, and consequently they are lifelong learners and doers of mathematics. The Conference Board of the Mathematical Sciences (CBMS 2012) has emphasized the importance of teachers of mathematics, at all levels, continuing to deepen their mathematical knowledge for teaching throughout their careers. These efforts provide teachers with natural opportunities to collaborate with mathematicians and mathematics educators (i.e., higher education faculty charged with the content and pedagogical education of teachers). Mathematics teachers' continual growth can be enhanced when they interact with mathematicians and mathematics educators in analyzing instructional and curricular issues (CBMS 2012). The Mathematics and Science Partnerships established by the National Science Foundation and the U.S. Department of Education stand as examples of collaborations among teachers, mathematicians, and mathematics educators, illustrating the potential of such collaborations to improve teachers' practice, their understanding of mathematical knowledge for teaching, and their students' learning (Mathematical Sciences Research Institute 2009).

Obstacles

In too many schools, professional isolation severely undermines attempts to increase collaboration among colleagues, both between teaching peers internally in the school and among teachers, mathematicians, and mathematics educators externally (Scholastic and the Bill & Melinda Gates Foundation, 2012). Such isolation stands as an obstacle to ensuring mathematical success for all students as well as teachers' continual growth. Unfortunately, some teachers actually embrace the norms of isolation and autonomy (Hattie 2012). A danger in isolation is that it can lead teachers to develop inconsistencies in their practice that in turn can create inequities in student learning, contributing to existing learning differentials (Ferrini-Mundy et. al. 1998). By contrast, research indicates not only more growth in mathematics achievement in students whose teachers regularly collaborate than in students whose teachers work in isolation, but also a reduction in traditional learning gaps among disaggregated groups (Moller et al. 2013).

To build a culture of professionalism, and to promote mathematical success for all students, the norm of teacher isolation must give way to a new professional norm of collaboration. It must become the norm for teachers to believe that they have a professional responsibility to collaborate with their colleagues and open their practice to collective observation, study, and improvement (NCTM 2007). One way to accomplish this vision is through participation in professional teacher organizations. National, state or provincial, and local professional communities allow for significant networking through attendance at conferences and institutes, as well as through the publication of journals and books. As Stigler and Hiebert (1999, p. 179) have suggested,

> The star teachers of the twenty-first century will be those who work together to infuse the best ideas into standard practice. They will be teachers who collaborate to build a system that has the goal of improving students' learning in the "average" classroom, who work to gradually improve standard classroom practices.... The star teachers of the twenty-first century will be teachers who work every day to improve teaching—not only their own but that of the whole profession.

A lack of time is one of the greatest challenges that teachers and administrators face in schools (White 2011), and limited time clearly stands as an obstacle to creating collaborative structures and reducing teacher isolation. Time during the school day is often inadequate for collaboration. Far too many teachers are provided with no, or very few and limited, opportunities to collaborate (Scholastic and the Bill & Melinda Gates Foundation 2012). Planning and problem solving tend to be done individually, and a spirit of professional autonomy often squelches any acknowledgment of the professional collaboration needed to strengthen professional practice. Daily schedules in most schools do not build in time for teams of grade-level or subject-based teachers to share, collaborate, or strengthen their mathematical pedagogical skills or deepen their understanding of mathematics. Even when time is allocated for teachers to collaborate in professional learning communities, the time is often too limited and is scheduled too irregularly to promote the type of sustained professional development, focused on mathematics and how to teach it, which is necessary to improve student learning (Blank and de las Alas 2009). Challenges related to time must be addressed and overcome if mathematics teachers are to ensure mathematical success for all students.

The current structure of professional development often stands as an obstacle to the development of a culture of professionalism. Teachers frequently feel as though professional development is something done *to* them, instead of something done *for* them, involving them as active partners in their own professional growth. Too much of what currently is offered to teachers as professional development has limited value and makes little impact on their pedagogical knowledge, their practice, or their students' achievement (Garet et al. 2010). A report from the Center for American Progress (DeMonte 2013) indicates that this lack of value and impact may be due to the fact that current professional development is frequently "short-term, episodic, and disconnected" (p. 1).

Effective professional development programs promote the growth of mathematics teachers in four major areas (see Doerr, Goldsmith, and Lewis [2010] for additional details):

- Teachers' mathematical knowledge and their capacity to use it in practice
- Teachers' capacity to notice, analyze, and respond to students' thinking
- Teachers' beliefs and dispositions that foster their continued learning
- Teachers' collegial relationships and learning structures that can support and sustain their learning

Research evidence indicates several features of high-quality professional development programs that support these goals (Blank and de las Alas 2009; Doerr, Goldsmith, and Lewis 2010):

- Substantial time investment over a sustained period (i.e., six months or more)
- Systemic support for teachers' learning (i.e., administrative support and coherence with other school initiatives)

- Opportunities for teachers to participate in active learning
- Opportunities for teachers to study the mathematics underlying the curriculum that they teach

The following table compares some unproductive and productive beliefs in the area of professionalism. It is important to note that these beliefs should not be viewed as good or bad, but rather as productive when they support effective teaching and learning or unproductive when they limit teachers' access to knowledge of and support to implement effective teaching practices.

Beliefs about professionalism in mathematics education	
Unproductive beliefs	**Productive beliefs**
Teachers arrive from teacher preparation programs prepared to be effective teachers.	Developing expertise as a mathematics teacher is a career-long process. The knowledge base of effective mathematics teaching and learning is continually expanding.
A deep understanding of mathematics content is sufficient for effective teaching.	Teachers of mathematics continue to learn throughout their careers in the areas of mathematical knowledge for teaching, mathematical pedagogical knowledge, and knowledge of students as learners of mathematics.
Effective teachers can work autonomously and in isolation. As long as the students in one's own classroom are successful, all is well.	Teachers who collaborate with colleagues inside and outside their school are more effective. All mathematics teachers are collectively responsible for student learning, the improvement of the professional knowledge base, and everyone's effectiveness.
Instructional coaching is unnecessary and a luxury in a school's budget. However, novice teachers might benefit from some general coaching support.	All professionals, even experienced teachers, can benefit from content-focused instructional coaching.
Teachers should be in direct contact with students for all or almost all of each school day.	A priority for schools and districts is to establish regular content-focused collaborative planning time for teachers at the same grade level or teachers of the same course and to schedule time periodically for vertical articulation.

Beliefs about professionalism in mathematics education, *continued*	
Unproductive beliefs	Productive beliefs
Highly effective teachers have an innate and natural ability to provide innovative instruction that results in high levels of student achievement.	Highly effective teachers become master teachers over time by continually improving their mathematical knowledge for teaching, mathematical pedagogical skills, and knowledge of students as learners of mathematics.
The textbook and digital resources provide all the necessary lesson plans and activities, so teachers have no need to engage in detailed unit and lesson planning.	Effective mathematics teaching results from purposeful planning. Highly effective teachers collaborate to design detailed mathematics lessons and then reflect on the effectiveness of those plans for student learning, in a cycle of continuous improvement.

Overcoming the obstacles

Two approaches used by high-performing school systems to support teachers' continual growth and ensure mathematical success for all students are to provide time for collaboration among teachers and to place coaches in schools to support teachers in implementing effective instructional practices (Barber and Mourshed 2007).

Collaborating on instruction

One structure that is designed to secure collaboration time for teachers is the professional learning community. Schmoker (2006) noted that "professional learning communities have emerged as arguably the best, most agreed-upon means by which to continuously improve instruction and student performance ... [T]he concurrence of the research community on this approach is quite remarkable" (p. 106). Specific approaches and protocols for implementing professional learning communities exist (Allison et al. 2010; DuFour et al. 2006; Kanold and Larson 2012; Perry 2011), but the most important consideration is not the specific type or approach taken to collaboration but the manner in which it is implemented. Teachers in effective professional learning communities—

- examine and prioritize the mathematics content and mathematical practices that students are to learn;

- develop and use common assessments to determine whether students have learned the agreed-on content and related mathematical practices;

- use data to drive continual reflection and instructional decisions;

- set both long-term and short-term instructional goals;

- discuss, select, and implement common research-informed instructional strategies and plans;

- develop action plans that they can implement when students demonstrate that they have or have not attained the standards; and

- have opportunities for continual learning, including mathematical knowledge for teaching, mathematical pedagogical skill, and knowledge of students as learners of mathematics.

Teacher collaboration does not automatically lead to professional learning or instructional improvement. Too often collaboration is characterized by little more than the sharing of materials or the swapping of stories (Stein, Russell, and Smith 2011). The evidence suggests that teachers may need up to three years to begin to work together effectively and move beyond mere cooperation to true collaboration (Perry and Lewis 2010). Professional learning communities must focus on issues related to pedagogy and student achievement and explore how teachers can work together toward common goals.

Effective instruction rests in part on careful instructional planning. Teachers' co-planning of lessons provides one of the greatest opportunities for making a positive difference on student learning (Hattie 2012; Morris, Hiebert, and Spitzer 2009). In some cultures (e.g., East Asian countries such as Japan) mathematics teachers devote significant time to planning lessons, and they collaboratively prepare detailed and lengthy lesson plans (Cheng 2011). In the United States, by contrast, it is the typical practice of teachers to spend relatively little time developing mathematics lesson plans (Ding and Carlson 2013). To improve instruction and ensure the mathematical success of all students, this practice of limited and isolated instructional planning must be eliminated and replaced with a practice of allocating time for collaborative planning.

Effective mathematics teachers not only collaborate but also focus their collaborative efforts on improving instruction and student learning through the co-planning of lessons. Focusing teachers' work within professional learning communities on detailed lesson planning has been demonstrated to be a highly productive strategy to support more in-depth interactions within collaborative communities and effect change in teachers' practice (Perry and Lewis 2010; Stein, Russell, and Smith 2011). Many teachers express concern that they do not have the time to devote to detailed lesson planning for every lesson that they teach. However, the perceived lack of time to devote careful planning to and reflection on *all* lessons cannot be used as an excuse *never* to collaboratively learn, plan, and reflect on the effectiveness of key lessons (Kanold and Larson 2012).

Teachers should be continually working with others at the same grade levels or in the same courses, as well as engaging in ongoing dialogue across grades or courses with those who teach mathematics to students in grades or courses above and below their own. It is essential that time be set aside to ensure that teachers throughout schools and districts possess a shared vision of the learning progressions of all students, with respect to both mathematical content and mathematical practices. In smaller school districts, electronic communications, including blogs and social media, can be used to connect teachers who might otherwise feel isolated because of school size or geography.

Teaching is a complex and harried profession, and all too often as a result teachers do not take the time necessary to engage in structured reflection. Instead, at best, they focus on finding quick fixes to immediate problems without addressing the more important and long-term learning needs of students (Korthagen and Vasalos 2010). However, reflection is critical, and NCTM (2007) has argued that the essential factor in the growth and improvement of teaching is not just lesson preparation, but also the *analysis of lesson outcomes* during and after each lesson. The degree to which teachers' instructional practice improves depends in part on how well and how frequently they reflect on their instructional practice (Artzt, Armour-Thomas, and Curcio 2011).

To improve instructional practice, teachers need to devote more time not only to collaborative planning but also to intentional and structured reflection. Lesson study is one structured method for collaboratively designing and reflecting on lessons (see Fernandez and Yoshida 2004; Lewis 2002). Another strategy to provide more structured reflection is the use of video data (Marzano et al. 2012). Many performance assessments for teaching— used for both initial licensure and mentoring—require digital videotaping and reflecting on classroom teaching episodes. Although teachers sometimes find the experience of watching themselves uncomfortable at first, they quickly discover that watching and critiquing instruction with colleagues by using video clips can be one of the most effective ways to promote reflection, growth, and learning (Artz et al. 2011; Marzano et al. 2012). Furthermore, the use of video-recorded lessons and reflection breaks down the cultural practice of teaching as an isolated practice and promotes a sense of collective responsibility for improving professional practice (Hiebert et al. 2003).

Coaching support

As important as it is that mathematics teachers collaborate to promote instructional improvement and their continual growth as professionals, it is also useful that they seek and draw support from an instructional coach who serves as a support resource or mentor. A mathematics instructional coach or specialist "is an individual who is well versed in mathematics content and pedagogy and who works directly with classroom teachers to improve student learning in mathematics" (Hull, Balka, and Harbin Miles 2009, p. 3).

Many highly effective professionals in a variety of fields seek coaching support to continually grow and improve (Knight 2007). Although there is a tendency to treat instructional coaches as a luxury, instructional coaching can be a highly effective strategy to improve professional performance (Gawande 2011). Teachers who receive coaching are more likely to implement new teaching strategies (McGatha 2009; Wei et al. 2009; Tschannen-Moran and McMaster 2009), and effective coaching can have a positive impact on student learning (Campbell and Malkus 2011).

Coaching is a critical component in supporting the implementation of effective teaching practices. Providing, supporting, and involving mathematics coaches or specialists are not luxuries if the goal of the school or district is to ensure mathematical success for all students. Mathematics teachers must be open to working collaboratively not only with their peers but also with an instructional mathematics coach or specialist who assists them as they continue to enhance their own knowledge of mathematics content and pedagogy and improve the achievement of their students.

Illustration

The following example shows the potential of a collaborative teaching team to support teachers' continuing professional growth and deepen students' learning and understanding of mathematics:

> A collaborative learning team of third-grade teachers is meeting during the teachers' biweekly mathematics planning time after school. Although the team does not have release time for professional learning community work, the teachers have made a commitment to meet every other week after school to collaboratively plan mathematics lessons, reflect on their effectiveness, and work to improve their own understanding of mathematics and mathematics pedagogy. This is the fifth in a series of meetings that the team has dedicated to planning lessons on connecting multiplication and division concepts.
>
> The teachers selected this topic as one of five to make the focus of in-depth planning this year. They based their selection of connections between multiplication and division concepts on student performance in previous years and the challenges that they have experienced in teaching this topic in the past. The teachers have hypothesized that students do not understand the underlying concepts and rely on rote procedures and that this lack of understanding contributes to their difficulty in relating these concepts. The team has recognized that to deepen their students' understanding, they too need to develop a deeper understanding of the concepts.
>
> To deepen their own understanding of the mathematics underlying this topic, the teachers decided at the beginning of the year to read *Developing Essential Understanding*

of Multiplication and Division for Teaching Mathematics in Grades 3–5 (Otto et al. 2011). At their second and third meetings, the team members discussed the book, focusing particularly on the third chapter, which addresses learning and teaching beginning division concepts and the relationship between multiplication and division.

This reading and the resulting discussion deepened the teachers' understanding of multiplication and division and sparked a constructive discussion that extended over the fourth session and now shapes the fifth session, where the teachers are considering new instructional tasks, representations, and discussion prompts that they can use in two ways: to engage students in developing an understanding of division from their understanding of multiplication and to check to be sure that students are developing this understanding as the lesson unfolds.

By the time the team members finish their fifth meeting on this topic, they have written an in-depth lesson plan (six pages in length) to introduce division as an extension of multiplication, including tasks and examples, key questions, anticipated student responses and their own replies, guided practice tasks, summary questions, academic language required in the lesson, adaptations for English language learners and students with disabilities, and formative assessment tasks that will help them determine whether students have made progress toward the established mathematics learning goals.

The members of the team commit to using the collaboratively planned lesson with their students, and they agree to come together to watch a video of one team member teaching the lesson at their next meeting. The team plans to devote its next meeting to discussing the effectiveness of the collaboratively designed lesson, which they will evaluate on the basis of student performance so that they can both plan necessary responses to student learning and refine the lesson, improving it for future use.

Moving to action

Building a culture of professionalism is challenging but possible. It is important to recognize that teaching is a cultural activity and that cultural activities resist change (Stigler and Thompson 2009). Building a culture of professional collaboration will therefore take time. The process of creating a new cultural norm of professional collaboration, openness of practice, and continual learning and improvement can begin in various ways. Grade-level or course teams may make a commitment to create common end-of-unit assessments with the goal of ensuring that all team members have the same expectations for students' learning in each unit. Or the growth of a new norm of professional collaboration may begin with a single team of grade-level or subject-based mathematics teachers making a commitment to work together on a single lesson plan after school, as the team in the preceding illustration did. Gradually, as trust builds among team members, the team members can begin to observe one another and reflect on lessons. Then they can design, plan, and reflect on more lessons, and begin to partner with local mathematicians or mathematics educators to deepen their understanding of mathematics and improve their practice.

As mathematics teachers demonstrate the positive impact of such collaboration on student learning, teachers should arrange to meet with building and district leaders to demonstrate the benefits of increased collaboration and coaching support. In collaboration, teachers, administrators, and other district leaders should make the case for more substantial structural and policy changes to enhance professionalism in their schools.

Taking Action

L
ike all written documents, *Principles to Actions* is merely words. These words will remain only ideas on paper or screen until they compel us all to action. Beliefs will remain unproductive and obstacles will continue to thwart progress until we collectively and collaboratively confront them and take the actions required for solving and overcoming these challenges.

This concluding section makes the case that all of us who are stakeholders have a role to play and important actions to take if we are finally to recognize our critical need for a world where the mathematics education of our students draws from research, is informed by common sense and good judgment, and is driven by a nonnegotiable belief that we must develop mathematical understanding and self-confidence in *all* students.

We need to take action to ensure that all students become confident in their ability to learn and use mathematics. Students must view themselves as capable of using their growing mathematical understanding to make sense of new problems situated in the world around them. Such students are aware of the cultural, historical, and scientific evolution of mathematics, and appreciate the role of mathematics in the development of our contemporary society. They seek relationships among mathematics and the disciplines that use its tools: the physical and life sciences, the social sciences, and the humanities. Such students believe that mathematics makes sense, appreciate mathematics as a field of study, and are willing to consider the possibilities for further studies in mathematics or mathematics-based fields.

We need to take action to create classrooms and learning environments where *students* are actively engaged with worthwhile tasks that promote mathematical understanding, problem solving, and reasoning. These students are working collaboratively as well as independently, using a range of concrete, print, and technological resources. They are interacting with one another and with their teacher, and they are focused on making sense of mathematics, comparing varied approaches to solving problems, and defending, confirming, verifying, or rejecting possible solutions. They are learning in classrooms that reflect our technological age, offering digital tools that allow teachers to take learning much deeper than ever before.

We need to take action to create classrooms where all students become mathematical problem solvers, making sense of problems and discussing their solutions. In such classrooms, students may work on problems that take hours or even days to solve—mirroring challenging, multifaceted problems in the world for which we are preparing them. They work cooperatively with their classmates on such realistic and complex problems, using varied solution paths and often finding more than one logically justifiable solution. They are comfortable using mathematics, understand the power of mathematical thinking, and can relate mathematics to meaningful contexts.

What will it take to create such classrooms in every school and district?

Leaders and Policymakers in All Districts and States or Provinces

Creating effective classrooms and learning environments for all students will take *leaders and policymakers in all districts and states or provinces, including commissioners, superintendents, and other central office administrators*, who are dedicated to ensuring that all teachers have the resources and support that are essential to enacting the Mathematics Teaching Practices for effective teaching and learning. Such leaders and policymakers understand that their policies, programs, and actions must result in the empowerment of teachers and principals. They are focused on ensuring that principals have the knowledge and tools to promote and support meaningful mathematics teaching and learning, including the purposeful use of assessment; that teachers have the knowledge and tools to plan and implement powerful mathematics lessons; and that students have the opportunity to become proficient with mathematical knowledge and confident in their ability to learn and make sense of mathematics. Such leaders and policymakers ensure that sufficient time is allocated, adequate resources are provided, and productive policies are enacted to ensure that every student has access to the opportunities and supports that he or she needs to succeed in mathematics. They understand the devastating impact of professional isolation and create collaborative structures to maximize professional growth, and they support risk taking and encourage new approaches that advance student learning.

Thus, leaders and policymakers in all districts and states or provinces, including commissioners, superintendents, and other central office administrators, must take the following actions:

For the Teaching and Learning Principle:

- Make ongoing professional development that supports the implementation of the eight Mathematics Teaching Practices a priority.

- Communicate the value of the Mathematics Teaching Practices to parents and the community and all educational stakeholders.

- Align accountability measures for teachers and principals with the Mathematics Teaching Practices.

For the Access and Equity Principle:

- Allocate resources to ensure that all students are provided with an appropriate amount of instructional time to maximize their learning potential.

- Ensure that teachers at all levels are emphasizing the mathematical practices as a key element of their instruction for all students.

- Eliminate the tracking of low-achieving students and instead structure interventions that provide high-quality instruction and other classroom support, such as math coaches and specialists.

- Provide support structures, co-curricular activities, and resources to increase the numbers of students from all racial, ethnic, gender, and socioeconomic groups who attain the highest levels of mathematics achievement.

For the Curriculum Principle:

- Ensure that the mathematics curriculum reflects the importance of the mathematical practices and supports and promotes conceptual understanding, procedural fluency, and their application to solving real-world problems.

For the Tools and Technology Principle:

- Incorporate and support the effective use of appropriate tools and technology in mathematics curriculum standards across all grade levels.

- Examine what mathematics should be taught, regularly reviewing the relevance of required topics in light of technology and considering other topics that may be required.

- Regularly review the possibilities for using technology to enhance teacher productivity and student learning.

For the Assessment Principle:

- Align assessments with the goals of the mathematics program by measuring students' conceptual understanding and proficiency in the mathematical practices.

- Create structures to ensure that the results of all assessments are used to strengthen teaching, curriculum, and support for students.

For the Professionalism Principle:

- Allocate resources for the staffing of mathematics instructional coaches or specialists in schools.

- Allocate time, support, and resources for consistent opportunities for professional learning communities and other collaborative structures for teachers of mathematics.

- Base decisions about licensing teachers, evaluating teachers, or student course placement on evidence from multiple measures.

What else will it take to create such classrooms in every school and district?

Principals, Coaches, Specialists, and Other School Leaders

Creating effective classrooms and learning environments in every school and district will take *principals, coaches, specialists, and other school leaders* who are committed to supporting teachers in their efforts to engage students in important mathematics and who fully understand the eight Mathematics Teaching Practices for effective instruction and assist teachers in consistently planning and implementing them. Such educators are knowledgeable about the families and communities from which students come and use this knowledge to help teachers determine instructional strategies and resources that provide the best support to help students learn the mathematics in the content expectations and develop proficiency with the mathematical processes in the practice expectations for each grade or course. These educators support improvement with multifaceted assessments used to monitor progress and inform changes to instruction, and they ensure professional interaction among teachers through a range of collaborative structures that focus on the teaching and learning of mathematics. They make the mathematical success of every student a nonnegotiable priority. Like their colleagues, these educators are dedicated professionals, possessing the necessary knowledge and skill to create opportunities that maximize the learning of mathematics. They support risk taking and encourage new approaches that advance student learning.

Thus, principals, coaches, specialists and other school leaders must take the following actions:

For the Teaching and Learning Principle:

- Make the eight Mathematics Teaching Practices a schoolwide focus that is expected for all teachers to strengthen learning and teaching for all students.

- Provide professional development and training that makes the implementation of the Mathematics Teaching Practices a priority.

- Observe lessons or engage in classroom walkthroughs, using the Mathematics Teaching Practices as the focus.

For the Access and Equity Principle:

- Consider teacher assignment practices to ensure that struggling students have access to effective mathematics teaching that incorporates the Mathematics Teaching Practices.

- Maintain a schoolwide culture with high expectations and a growth mindset.

- Develop and implement high-quality interventions.

- Ensure that curricular and extracurricular resources are available to support and challenge all students.

For the Curriculum Principle:

- Allocate time for collaborative interactions among mathematics teachers to study the school's curriculum—at, above, and below the intended grade level or course.

- Ensure that curriculum maps and pacing guides are flexible and serve as a resource for mathematics teachers, providing a general sequence and timeline but allowing reasonable variation in pacing to meet students' needs.

- Ensure that the process of selecting textbooks and other instructional materials is a collaborative process that includes careful examination of the degree to which the textbooks not only align with the standards but also develop topics coherently within and across grades, promote the mathematical practices, and support effective instruction as characterized by the Mathematics Teaching Practices.

For the Tools and Technology Principle:

- Ensure that teachers of mathematics receive mathematics-specific professional development on technology and its connection with curriculum and instruction.

- Expect and encourage mathematics teachers to actively implement the use of instructional technology and physical materials and to reflect that expectation in classroom assessments.

- Establish criteria for the selection of textbooks and instructional materials that include regular and effective use of technology.

For the Assessment Principle:

- Make collaborative design and implementation of common formative assessment processes a norm, and allocate the necessary time for grade-level or subject-based teacher teams to complete this work.

- Provide teachers with the professional development support that they need to develop their assessment expertise.

- Ensure that collaborative teams use assessment results appropriately to guide and modify instructional practices and make program improvements.

For the Professionalism Principle:

- Provide appropriate and ongoing opportunities for professional growth and development for teachers, including coaching and collaborative planning opportunities that build capacity to implement the Mathematics Teaching Practices.

- Allocate time for teachers to collaborate in professional learning communities.

- Maintain a culture of continual improvement, learning, and collaboration.

- Support the staffing of mathematics coaches, specialists, and instructional leaders.

- Support sustained professional development that engages teachers in continual growth of their mathematical knowledge for teaching, pedagogical content knowledge, and knowledge of students as learners of mathematics.

What else will it take to create such classrooms in every school and district?

Teachers

Most important, creating effective classrooms and learning environments for all students in every school and district will take *teachers* who plan and implement effective instruction as described by the Mathematics Teaching Principles. Such teachers establish clear goals for the mathematics that their students will learn, and select a progression of coherent activities and problems that align with those goals. They use questioning effectively to assess and advance student understanding, provide opportunities for productive struggle, and facilitate discourse to foster conceptual understanding and procedural fluency. They use mathematical representations to support students' learning and collect and use evidence of students' thinking to modify and improve instruction. They know and use the cultural and linguistic resources of their students to create learning environments that build on and extend these resources, ensuring that learning is connected with students' sense of mathematical identity. They work collaboratively with colleagues to plan instruction, solve common challenges, and provide mutual support as they take collective responsibility for student learning.

Thus, teachers of mathematics must take the following actions:

For the Teaching and Learning Principle:

- Consistently implement the eight Mathematics Teaching Practices.

- Elicit, value, and celebrate varied approaches and solution paths that students take to solve mathematics problems, explain their thinking, and critique the arguments of others.

- Give priority to the mathematical practices, including problem solving, reasoning, and constructing viable arguments in every aspect of classroom practice—including teaching, assessment, curriculum decisions, and the use of tools and technology.

- Plan and implement units and lessons that promote positive dispositions toward the study of mathematics, including curiosity, self-confidence, flexibility, and perseverance.

For the Access and Equity Principle:

- Develop socially, emotionally, and academically safe environments for mathematics teaching and learning—environments in which students feel safe to engage with one another and with teachers.

- Understand and use the social contexts, cultural backgrounds, and identities of students as resources to foster access, motivate students to learn more mathematics, and engage student interest.

- Model high expectations for each student's success in problem solving, reasoning, and understanding.

- Promote the development of a growth mindset among students.

For the Curriculum Principle:

- Use a variety of high-quality print and online resources to carefully plan units and lessons based on the Mathematics Teaching Practices.

- Become familiar with the content standards through reading and reflecting on the main ideas of the standards and the learning progressions that students follow.

- Engage in dialogue with colleagues who teach other mathematics courses or grade levels to understand the intended curriculum from both horizontal and vertical perspectives.

- Evaluate curricular materials and resources, including textbooks, collections of activities, and software, to determine the extent to which these materials align with the standards, ensure coherent development of topics within and across grades, promote the mathematical practices, and support effective instruction that implements the Mathematics Teaching Practices.

- Sequence tasks and activities with long-term goals in mind; when conducting lesson and unit planning, focus on connections among key mathematical ideas that are situated in real-world and mathematical contexts.

For the Tools and Technology Principle:

- Implement lessons that make use of technological investigations that precede or accompany the development of paper-and-pencil skills.

- Ensure that students see both the power and limitations of technology, and expect them to examine answers for reasonableness and applicability to the context and to choose appropriate tools for the task at hand.

- Incorporate mathematical tools and technology as an everyday part of the mathematics classroom, recognizing that students should experience "mathematical action technologies" and physical or virtual manipulatives to explore important mathematics.

- Plan carefully for the use of classroom technology to ensure that it builds student understanding and reasoning.

For the Assessment Principle:

- Work in collaborative grade-level or subject-based teams to develop common assessments to be used formatively; commit to their use, and analyze and apply the results to advance student learning and improve instruction.

- Evaluate students' mathematics learning on the basis of multiple measures to make more reliable and valid judgments about what students know and are able to do.

- Provide students with descriptive, accurate, and timely feedback on assessments, including strengths, weaknesses, and next steps for progress toward the learning targets.

- Recognize that effective instruction and ongoing review are the best high-stakes "test prep" strategies.

- View assessment results as supplying part of the picture of instructional effectiveness and use them to drive instructional decision making, focus personal professional growth, and make program improvements.

For the Professionalism Principle:

- Continually grow in knowledge of mathematics for teaching, mathematical pedagogical knowledge, and knowledge of students as learners of mathematics.

- Demand opportunities for professional development and collaboration that strengthen mathematics content knowledge and the implementation of the Mathematics Teaching Practices.

- Collaborate with colleagues on issues of *access and equity, curriculum, instruction, tools and technology, assessment,* and *professional growth.*

- Assume collective responsibility for the learning of all students in the school.

- Join and participate in local, state, or national professional organizations.

Every leader and policymaker, every school and district administrator, and every teacher, coach, and specialist of mathematics—in conjunction with all other stakeholders, from parents to community members—must make a commitment to these actions. Only when these words become actions and the actions lead to more productive beliefs, new norms of instructional practice, and the implementation of the essential supporting elements will we overcome the obstacles that currently prevent school mathematics from ensuring mathematical success for all students.

References

ACT. *Act 2013 Profile Report: Graduating Class 2013—National.* Iowa City, Iowa: ACT, 2013.

Aguirre, Julia Maria, Karen Mayfield-Ingram, and Danny Bernard Martin. *The Impact of Identity in K–8 Mathematics Learning and Teaching: Rethinking Equity-Based Practices.* Reston, Va.: National Council of Teachers of Mathematics, 2013.

Allensworth, Elaine, Macarena Correa, and Steve Ponisciak. *From High School to the Future: ACT Preparation—Too Much, Too Late: Why ACT Scores Are Low in Chicago and What It Means for Schools.* CCSR Research Report. Chicago: Consortium on Chicago School Research (CCSR), 2008.

Allison, Elle, Laura Besser, Lauren Campsen, Juan Córdova, Brandon Doubek, Linda Gregg, Connie Kamm, et al. *Data Teams: The Big Picture Looking at Data Teams through a Collaborative Lens.* Englewood, Colo.: Lead and Learn Press, 2010.

American Diploma Project. *Ready or Not: Creating a High School Diploma That Counts.* Washington, D.C.: Achieve, 2004.

Arcavi, Abraham. "The Role of Visual Representations in the Learning of Mathematics." *Educational Studies in Mathematics* 52, no. 3 (2003): 215–41.

Artzt, Alice F., Eleanor Armour-Thomas, and Frances R. Curcio. *Becoming a Reflective Mathematics Teacher: A Guide for Observations and Self-Assessment.* New York: Routledge, 2011.

Ashcraft, Mark H. "Math Anxiety: Personal, Educational, and Cognitive Consequences." *Current Directions in Psychological Science* 11, no. 5 (2002): 181–85.

Ball, Deborah Loewenberg, and Francesca M. Forzani. "Building a Common Core for Learning to Teach and Connecting Professional Learning to Practice." *American Educator* 35, no. 2 (2011): 17–21.

———. "Teaching Skillful Teaching." *Educational Leadership* 68, no. 4 (2010): 40–45.

Ball, Deborah Loewenberg, Laurie Sleep, Timothy A. Boerst, and Hyman Bass. "Combining the Development of Practice and the Practice of Development in Teacher Education." *Elementary School Journal* 109, no. 5 (2009): 458–74.

Ball, Deborah Loewenberg, Mark Hoover Thames, and Geoffrey Phelps. "Content Knowledge for Teaching: What Makes It Special?" *Journal of Teacher Education* 59, no. 5 (2008): 389–407.

Banilower, Eric R., Sally E. Boyd, Joan D. Pasley, and Iris R. Weiss. *Lessons from a Decade of Mathematics and Science Reform*. Chapel Hill, N.C.: Horizon Research, 2006.

Barber, Michael, and Mona Mourshed. *How the World's Best-Performing School Systems Come Out on Top*. London: McKinsey, 2007. http://www.mckinsey.com/client _service/social_sector/ latest_thinking/worlds_most_improved_schools.aspx.

Barkatsas, Anastasios Tasos, and John Malone. "A Typology of Mathematics Teachers' Beliefs about Teaching and Learning Mathematics and Instructional Practices." *Mathematics Education Research Journal* 17, no. 2 (2005): 69–90.

Baroody, Arthur J. "Mastering the Basic Number Combinations." *Teaching Children Mathematics* 13, no. 1 (2006): 23–31.

Baroody, Arthur J., Neet Priya Bajwa, and Michael Eiland. "Why Can't Johnny Remember the Basic Facts?" *Developmental Disabilities Research Reviews* 15, no. 1 (2009): 69–79.

Battey, Dan. "'Good' Mathematics Teaching for Students of Color and Those in Poverty: The Importance of Relational Interactions within Instruction." *Educational Studies in Mathematics* 82, no. 1 (2013): 125–44.

Battista, Michael T. "Conceptualizations and Issues Related to Learning Progressions, Learning Trajectories, and Levels of Sophistication." *Mathematics Enthusiast* 8, no. 3 (2011): 507–70.

Berry, Robert Q., III, and Mark W. Ellis. "Multidimensional Teaching." *Mathematics Teaching in the Middle School* 19, no. 3 (2013): 172–78.

Biafora, Frank, and Ansalone, George. "Perceptions and Attitudes of School Principals towards School Tracking: Structural Considerations of Personal Beliefs." *Education* 128, no. 4 (2008): 588–602.

Black, Paul, and Dylan Wiliam. "Inside the Black Box: Raising Standards through Classroom Assessment." *Phi Delta Kappan* 80, no. 1 (1998a): 139–48.

———. "Assessment and Classroom Learning." *Assessment in Education* 5, no. 1 (1998b): 7–74.

Blackwell, Lisa S., Kali H. Trzesniewski, and Carol Sorich Dweck. "Implicit Theories of Intelligence Predict Achievement across an Adolescent Transition: A Longitudinal Study and an Intervention." *Child Development* 78, no. 1 (2007): 246–63.

Blank, Rolf K., and Nina de las Alas. *Effects of Teacher Professional Development on Gains in Student Achievement: How Meta Analysis Provides Scientific Evidence Useful to Education Leaders*. Washington, D.C.: Council of Chief State School Officers, 2009.

Boaler, Jo. *Experiencing School Mathematics: Teaching Styles, Sex, and Setting*. Buckingham, UK: Open University Press, 1997.

———. "How a Detracked Mathematics Approach Promoted Respect, Responsibility, and High Achievement." *Theory into Practice* 45, no. 1 (2006): 40–46.

———. *What's Math Got to Do with It? Helping Children Learn to Love Their Least Favorite Subject—and Why It's Important for America.* New York: Penguin, 2008.

———. "Changing Students' Lives through the De-Tracking of Urban Mathematics Classrooms." *Journal of Urban Mathematics Education* 4, no. 1 (2011): 7–14.

Boaler, Jo, and Karin Brodie. "The Importance, Nature, and Impact of Teacher Questions." In *Proceedings of the 26th Annual Meeting of the North American Chapter of the International Group for the Psychology of Mathematics Education,* vol. 2, pp. 773–81. Toronto: Ontario Institute for Studies in Education of the University of Toronto, 2004.

Boaler, Jo, and Megan Staples. "Creating Mathematical Futures through an Equitable Teaching Approach: The Case of Railside School." *Teachers College Record* 110, no. 3 (2008): 608–45.

Bransford, John D., Ann L. Brown, and Rodney R. Cocking, eds. *How People Learn: Brain, Mind, Experience, and School.* Expanded ed. National Research Council Committee on Developments in the Science of Learning and Committee on Learning Research and Educational Practice. Washington, D.C.: National Academy Press, 2000.

Bray, Wendy S. "How to Leverage the Potential of Mathematical Errors." *Teaching Children Mathematics* 19, no. 7 (2013): 424–31.

Burris, Carol Corbett, Jay P. Heubert, and Henry M. Levin. "Accelerating Mathematics Achievement Using Heterogeneous Grouping." *American Educational Research Journal* 43, no. 1 (2006): 137–54.

Burris, Carol Corbett, Ed Wiley, Kevin Welner, and John Murphy. "Accountability, Rigor, and Detracking: Achievement Effects of Embracing a Challenging Curriculum as a Universal Good for All Students." *Teachers College Record* 110, no. 3 (2008): 571–607.

Bush, William S., Diane J. Briars, Jere Confrey, Kathleen Cramer, Carl Lee, W. Gary Martin, Michael Mays, et al. *Common Core State Standards (CCSS) Mathematics Curriculum Materials Analysis Project,* 2011. http://www.mathedleadership.org/ccss /materials.html.

Campbell, Patricia F. "Empowering Children and Teachers in the Elementary Mathematics Classrooms of Urban Schools." *Urban Education* 30, no. 4 (1996): 449–75.

Campbell, Patricia F., and Nathaniel N. Malkus. "The Impact of Elementary Mathematics Coaches on Student Achievement." *Elementary School Journal* 111, no. 3 (2011): 430–54.

Carpenter, Thomas P., Elizabeth Fennema, Megan Loef Franke, Linda Levi, and Susan B. Empson. *Children's Mathematics: Cognitively Guided Instruction.* Portsmouth, N.H.: Heinemann, 1999.

Carpenter, Thomas P., Elizabeth Fennema, Penelope L. Peterson, Chi-Pang Chiang, and Megan Loef. "Using Knowledge of Children's Mathematics Thinking in Classroom Teaching: An Experimental Study." *American Educational Research Journal* 26 (Winter 1989): 499–531.

Carpenter, Thomas P., Megan Loef Franke, and Linda Levi. *Thinking Mathematically: Integrating Arithmetic and Algebra in Elementary Schools.* Portsmouth, N.H.: Heinemann, 2003.

Carter, Susan. "Disequilibrium and Questioning in the Primary Classroom: Establishing Routines That Help Students Learn." *Teaching Children Mathematics* 15, no. 3 (2008): 134–37.

Chamberlin, Michelle T. "Teachers' Discussions of Students' Thinking: Meeting the Challenge of Attending to Students' Thinking." *Journal of Mathematics Teacher Education* 8, no. 2 (2005): 141–70.

Chapin, Suzanne H., and Catherine O'Connor. "Academically Productive Talk: Supporting Students' Learning in Mathematics." In *The Learning of Mathematics,* Sixty-ninth Yearbook of the National Council of Teachers of Mathematics (NCTM), edited by W. Gary Martin and Marilyn Strutchens, pp. 113–39. Reston, Va.: NCTM, 2007.

Charles, Randall I. "Big Ideas and Understandings as the Foundation for Elementary and Middle School Mathematics." *Journal of Mathematics Education Leadership* 7, no. 1 (2005): 9–24.

Cheng, Kai-ming. "Shanghai: How a Big City in a Developing Country Leaped to the Head of the Class." In *Surpassing Shanghai: An Agenda for American Education Built on the World's Leading Systems,* edited by Marc S. Tucker, pp. 21–50. Cambridge, Mass.: Harvard University Press, 2011.

Clarke, Shirley. *Enriching Feedback in the Primary Classroom.* London: Hodder and Stoughton, 2003.

Clarke, Shirley, Helen Timperley, and John Hattie. *Unlocking Formative Assessment: Practical Strategies for Enhancing Students' Learning in the Primary and Intermediate Classroom.* Auckland, New Zealand: Hodder Moa Beckett, 2004.

Clements, Douglas H., and Julie Sarama. "Learning Trajectories in Mathematics Education." *Mathematical Thinking and Learning* 6, no. 2 (2004): 81–89.

Cohen, Jessica, and Karen F. Hollebrands. "Technology Tools to Support Mathematics Teaching." In *Focus in High School Mathematics: Technology to Support Reasoning and Sense Making,* edited by Thomas P. Dick and Karen F. Hollebrands, pp. 105–22. Reston, Va.: National Council of Teachers of Mathematics, 2011.

College Board. *College Board Standards for College Success: Mathematics and Statistics.* New York: College Board, 2006.

———. *2013 College-Bound Seniors: Total Group Profile Report.* New York: College Board, 2013a.

———. *2013 SAT Report on College and Career Readiness.* New York: College Board, 2013c.

———. *Student Score Distributions: AP Exams May 2013.* New York: College Board, 2013b. http://media.collegeboard.com/digitalServices/pdf/research/2013/STUDENT -SCORE-DISTRIBUTIONS-2013.pdf.

Collins, Jim. *Good to Great: Why Some Companies Make the Leap ... and Others Don't.* New York: HarperCollins, 2001.

Common Core State Standards Writing Team. "Progressions Documents for the Common Core Math Standards" (drafts, Institute for Mathematics and Education, University of Arizona, Tucson, 2013). http://ime.math.arizona.edu /progressions/.

Conference Board of the Mathematical Sciences (CBMS). *The Mathematical Education of Teachers II.* Providence, R.I.: American Mathematical Society; Washington D.C.: Mathematical Association of America, 2012.

Crespo, Sandra. "Seeing More than Right and Wrong Answers: Prospective Teachers' Interpretations of Students' Mathematical Work." *Journal of Mathematics Teacher Education* 3, no. 2 (2000): 155–81.

Crespo, Sandra, Andreas O. Kyriakides, and Shelly McGee. "Nothing Basic about Basic Facts." *Teaching Children Mathematics* 12, no. 2 (2005): 61–67.

Cross, D. I., R. A. Hudson, O. Adefope, M. Y. Lee, L. Rapacki, and A. Perez. "Success Made Probable: African-American Girls' Exploration in Statistics through Project-Based Learning." *Journal of Urban Mathematics Education* 5, no. 2 (2012): 55–86.

Darling-Hammond, Linda. "Third Annual Brown Lecture in Education Research—The Flat Earth and Education: How America's Commitment to Equity Will Determine Our Future." *Educational Researcher* 36, no. 6 (2007): 318–34.

Daro, Phil, Frederic A. Mosher, and Tom Corcoran. *Learning Trajectories in Mathematics: A Foundation for Standards, Curriculum, Assessment, and Instruction.* Philadelphia: Consortium for Policy Research in Education, 2011.

David, Jane D., and David Greene. *Improving Mathematics Instruction in Los Angeles High Schools: An Evaluation of the PRISMA Pilot Program.* Palo Alto, Calif.: Bay Area Research Group, 2007.

Delcourt, Marcia A. B., Brenda H. Loyd, Dewey G. Cornell, and Marc D. Goldberg. *Evaluation of the Effects of Programming Arrangements on Student Learning Outcomes.* Charlottesville, Va.: University of Virginia, 1994.

DeMonte, Jenny. *High-Quality Professional Development for Teachers: Supporting Teacher Training to Improve Student Learning.* Washington, D.C.: Center for American Progress, 2013.

Dick, Thomas P., and Karen F. Hollebrands. *Focus in High School Mathematics: Technology to Support Reasoning and Sense Making.* Reston, Va.: National Council of Teachers of Mathematics, 2011.

Dieker, Lisa A., Paula Maccini, Tricia K. Strickland, and Jessica H. Hunt. "Minimizing Weaknesses and Maximizing Strengths of Students with Disabilities." In *Focus in High School Mathematics: Fostering Reasoning and Sense Making for All Students*, edited by Marilyn E. Strutchens and Judith Reed Quander, pp. 37–63. Reston, Va.: National Council of Teachers of Mathematics, 2011.

Ding, Meixia, and Mary Alice Carlson. "Elementary Teachers' Learning to Construct High-Quality Mathematics Lesson Plans: A Use of IES Recommendations." *Elementary School Journal* 113, no. 3 (2013): 359–75.

Doerr, Helen M., Lynn T. Goldsmith, and Catherine C. Lewis. *Mathematics Professional Development Brief.* NCTM Research Brief. Reston, Va.: National Council of Teachers of Mathematics, 2010.

Donovan, M. Suzanne, and John D. Bransford, eds. *How Students Learn: History, Mathematics, and Science in the Classroom.* National Research Council, Committee on *How People Learn: A Targeted Report for Teachers.* Washington, D.C.: National Academies Press, 2005.

Dubinsky, Ed, and Robin T. Wilson. "High School Students' Understanding of the Function Concept." *The Journal of Mathematical Behavior* 32, no. 1 (2013): 83–101.

DuFour, Richard, Rebecca DuFour, Robert Eaker, and Thomas Many. *Learning by Doing: A Handbook for Professional Learning Communities at Work.* Bloomington, Ind.: Solution Tree Press, 2006.

Duit, Reinders, and David F. Treagust. "Conceptual Change: A Powerful Framework for Improving Science Teaching and Learning." *International Journal of Science Education* 25, no. 6 (2003): 671–88.

Dweck, Carol. *Mindset: The New Psychology of Success.* New York: Random House, 2006.

———. *Mindsets and Math/Science Achievement.* New York: Carnegie Corporation of New York Institute for Advanced Study, 2008.

Ellis, Mark. "Leaving No Child Behind Yet Allowing None Too Far Ahead: Ensuring (In)Equity in Mathematics Education through the Science of Measurement and Instruction." *Teachers College Record* 110, no. 6 (2008): 1330–56.

Ellis, Mark, and Robert Q. Berry III. "The Paradigm Shift in Mathematics Education: Explanations and Implications of Reforming Conceptions of Teaching and Learning." *The Mathematics Educator* 15, no. 1 (2005): 7–17.

Engle, Randi A., and Faith C. Conant. "Guiding Principles for Fostering Productive Disciplinary Engagement: Explaining an Emergent Argument in a Community of Learners Classroom." *Cognition and Instruction* 20, no. 4 (2002): 399–483.

Erlwanger, Stanley H. "Benny's Conception of Rules and Answers in IPI Mathematics." In *Classics in Mathematics Education Research*, edited by Thomas P. Carpenter, John A. Dossey, and Julie L. Koehler, pp. 48–58. Reston, Va.: National Council of Teachers of Mathematics, 2004.

Fernandez, Clea, and Makoto Yoshida. *Lesson Study: A Japanese Approach to Improving Mathematics Teaching and Learning*. Mahwah, N.J.: Erlbaum, 2004.

Ferrini-Mundy, Joan, Karen Graham, Loren Johnson, and Geoffrey Mills. *Making Change in Mathematics Education: Learning from the Field*. Reston, Va.: National Council of Teachers of Mathematics, 1998.

Flores, Alfinio. "Examining Disparities in Mathematics Education: Achievement Gap or Opportunity Gap?" *High School Journal* 91, no. 1 (2007): 29–42.

Fosnot, Catherine Twomey, and William Jacob. *Young Mathematicians at Work: Constructing Algebra*. Portsmouth, N.H.: Heinemann, 2010.

Franke, Meghan, Noreen M. Webb, Angela Chan, Dan Battey, Marsha Ing, Deanna Freund, and Tondra De. *Eliciting Student Thinking in Elementary School Mathematics Classrooms*. CRESST Report 725. Los Angeles: National Center for Research on Evaluation, Standards, and Student Testing, 2007.

Franklin, Christine, Gary Kader, Denise Mewborn, Jerry Moreno, Roxy Peck, Mike Perry, and Richard Scheaffer. *Guidelines for Assessment and Instruction in Statistics Education (GAISE) Report: A Pre-K Curriculum Framework*. Alexandria, Va.: American Statistical Association, 2007.

Fuson, Karen C. "Toward Computational Fluency in Multidigit Multiplication and Division." *Teaching Children Mathematics* 9, no. 6 (2003): 300–305.

Fuson, Karen C., and Sybilla Beckmann. "Standard Algorithms in the Common Core State Standards." *National Council of Supervisors of Mathematics Journal of Mathematics Education Leadership* 14, no. 1 (2012/2013): 14–30.

Fuson, Karen C., Mindy Kalchman, and John D. Bransford. "Mathematical Understanding: An Introduction." In *How Students Learn: History, Mathematics, and Science in the Classroom*, edited by M. Suzanne Donovan and John D. Bransford, Committee on How People Learn: A Targeted Report for Teachers, National Research Council, pp. 217–56. Washington, D.C.: National Academies Press, 2005.

Fuson, Karen C., and Aki Murata. "Integrating NRC Principles and the NCTM Process Standards to Form a Class Learning Path Model That Individualizes within Whole-Class Activities." *National Council of Supervisors of Mathematics Journal of Mathematics Education Leadership* 10, no. 1 (2007): 72–91.

Gamoran, Adam. "Tracking and Inequality: New Directions for Research and Practice." In *The Routledge International Handbook of the Sociology of Education*, edited by Michael W. Apple, Stephen J. Ball, and Luis Armando Gandin, pp. 213–28. New York: Routledge, 2010.

Garet, Michael S., Andrew J. Wayne, Fran Stancavage, James Taylor, Kirk Walters, Mengli Song, Seth Brown, et al. *Middle School Mathematics Professional Development Impact Study: Findings after the First Year of Implementation.* NCEE 2010-4009. Washington, D.C.: National Center for Education Evaluation and Regional Assistance, Institute of Education Sciences, U.S. Department of Education, 2010.

Gawande, Atul. "Annals of Medicine: Personal Best: Top Athletes and Singers Have Coaches, Should You?" *New Yorker.* October 3, 2011, 44–53.

Goodwin, Bryan, and Kirsten Miller. "Evidence on Flipped Classrooms Is Still Coming In." *Educational Leadership* 70, no. 6 (2013): 78–80.

Greeno, James G., and Rogers P. Hall. "Practicing Representation." *Phi Delta Kappan* 78, no. 5 (1997): 361–67.

Griffin, Sharon. "Laying the Foundation for Computational Fluency in Early Childhood." *Teaching Children Mathematics* 9, no. 6 (2003): 306–9.

———. "Fostering the Development of Whole-Number Sense: Teaching Mathematics in the Primary Grades." In *How Students Learn: History, Mathematics, and Science in the Classroom*, edited by M. Suzanne Donovan and John D. Bransford, Committee on How People Learn: A Targeted Report for Teachers, National Research Council, pp. 257–308. Washington, D.C.: National Academies Press, 2005.

Grossman, Pam, Karen Hammerness, and Morva McDonald. "Redefining Teaching, Re-imagining Teacher Education." *Teachers and Teaching: Theory and Practice* 15, no. 2 (2009): 273–89.

Gutiérrez, Rochelle. "Advancing African-American Urban Youth in Mathematics: Unpacking the Success of One Math Department." *American Journal of Education* 109, no. 1 (2000): 63–111.

———. "Enabling the Practice of Mathematics Teachers in Context: Towards a New Equity Research Agenda." *Mathematical Thinking and Learning* 4, no. 2/3 (2002): 145–87.

———. "The Sociopolitical Turn in Mathematics Education." *Journal for Research in Mathematics Education* 44, no. 1 (2013): 37–68.

Haladyna, Thomas M., and Steven M. Downing. "A Taxonomy of Multiple-Choice Item-Writing Rules." *Applied Measurement in Education* 2, no. 1 (1989): 37–50.

Handal, Boris. "Teachers' Mathematical Beliefs: A Review." *Mathematics Educator* 13, no. 2 (2003): 47–57.

Hattie, John A. C. *Visible Learning: A Synthesis of over 800 Meta-Analyses Relating to Achievement.* New York: Routledge, 2009.

———. *Visible Learning for Teachers: Maximizing Impact on Learning.* New York: Routledge, 2012.

Hattie, John, and Helen Timperley. "The Power of Feedback." *Review of Educational Research* 77, no. 1 (2007): 81–112.

Haystead, Mark W., and Robert J. Marzano. *Meta-Analytic Synthesis of Studies Conducted at Marzano Research Laboratory on Instructional Strategies.* Englewood, Colo.: Marzano Research Laboratory, 2009.

Herbel-Eisenmann, Beth A., and M. Lynn Breyfogle. "Questioning Our Patterns of Questioning." *Mathematics Teaching in the Middle School* 10, no. 9 (2005): 484–89.

Heritage, Margaret. *Learning Progressions: Supporting Instruction and Formative Assessment.* Washington, D.C.: Council of Chief State School Officers, 2008.

Herman, Joan, and Robert Linn. *On the Road to Assessing Deeper Learning: The Status of Smarter Balanced and PARCC Assessment Consortia.* CRESST Report 823. Los Angeles: University of California, National Center for Research on Evaluation, Standards, and Student Testing (CRESST), 2013.

Hiebert, James, Thomas P. Carpenter, Elizabeth Fennema, Karen C. Fuson, Diana Wearne, Hanlie Murray, Alwyn Olivier, and Piet Human. *Making Sense: Teaching and Learning Mathematics with Understanding.* Portsmouth, N.H.: Heinemann, 1997.

Hiebert, James, Ronald Gallimore, Helen Garnier, Karen Bogard Givvin, Hilary Hollingsworth, Jennifer Jacobs, Angel Miu-Ying Chui, et al. *Highlights from the TIMSS 1999 Video Study of Eighth-Grade Mathematics Teaching.* Washington, D.C.: U.S. Department of Education, National Center for Education Statistics, 2003.

Hiebert, James, and Douglas A. Grouws. "The Effects of Classroom Mathematics Teaching on Students' Learning." In *Second Handbook of Research on Mathematics Teaching and Learning*, edited by Frank K. Lester, Jr., pp. 371–404. Charlotte, N.C.: Information Age; Reston, Va.: National Council of Teachers of Mathematics, 2007.

Hiebert, James, Anne K. Morris, Dawn Berk, and Amanda Jansen. "Preparing Teachers to Learn from Teaching." *Journal of Teacher Education* 58, no. 1 (2007): 47–61.

Hiebert, James, and James W. Stigler. "A World of Difference." *Journal of Staff Development* 25, no. 4 (2004): 10–15.

Hiebert, James, and Diana Wearne. "Instructional Tasks, Classroom Discourse, and Students' Learning in Second-Grade Arithmetic." *American Educational Research Journal* 30, no. 2 (1993): 393–425.

Hill, Heather C., Merrie L. Blunk, Charalambos Y. Charalambous, Jennifer M. Lewis, Geoffrey C. Phelps, Laurie Sleep, and Deborah Loewenberg Ball. "Mathematical

Knowledge for Teaching and the Mathematical Quality of Instruction: An Exploratory Study." *Cognition and Instruction* 26, no. 4 (2008): 430–511.

Hill, Heather C., Brian Rowan, and Deborah Loewenberg Ball. "Effects of Teachers' Mathematical Knowledge for Teaching on Student Achievement." *American Educational Research Journal* 42, no. 2 (2005): 371–406.

Hlas, Anne Cummings, and Christopher S. Hlas. "A Review of High-Leverage Teaching Practices: Making Connections between Mathematics and Foreign Languages." *Foreign Language Annals* 45, no. s1 (2012): s76–s97.

Hogan, Maureen P. "The Tale of Two Noras: How a Yup'ik Middle Schooler Was Differently Constructed as a Math Learner." *Diaspora, Indigenous, and Minority Education* 2, no. 2 (2008): 90–114.

Horn, Ilana. *Strength in Numbers: Collaborative Learning in Secondary Mathematics.* Reston, Va.: National Council of Teachers of Mathematics, 2012.

Hoy, Wayne K., C. John Tarter, and Anita Woolfolk Hoy. "Academic Optimism of Schools: A Force for Student Achievement." *American Educational Research Journal* 43, no. 3 (2006): 425–46.

Hufferd-Ackles, Kimberly, Karen C. Fuson, and Miriam Gamoran Sherin. "Describing Levels and Components of a Math-Talk Learning Community." *Journal for Research in Mathematics Education* 35, no. 2 (2004): 81–116.

———. "Describing Levels and Components of a Math-Talk Learning Community." In *Lessons Learned from Research*, edited by Edward A. Silver and Patricia A. Kenney. Reston, Va.: National Council of Teachers of Mathematics, 2014.

Huinker, DeAnn. "Dimensions of Fraction Operation Sense." In *Defining Mathematics Education: Presidential Yearbook Selections 1926–2012,* Seventy-fifth Yearbook of the National Council of Teachers of Mathematics (NCTM), pp. 373-380. Reston, Va.: NCTM, 2013.

Hull, Ted H., Don S. Balka, and Ruth Harbin Miles. *A Guide to Mathematics Coaching: Processes for Increasing Student Achievement.* Thousand Oaks, Calif.: Corwin, 2009.

Isaacs, Andrew C., and William M. Carroll. "Strategies for Basic-Facts Instruction." *Teaching Children Mathematics* 5, no. 9 (1999): 508–15.

Jackson, Kara, Anne Garrison, Jonee Wilson, Lynsey Gibbons, and Emily Shahan. "Exploring Relationships between Setting Up Complex Tasks and Opportunities to Learn in Concluding Whole-Class Discussions in Middle-Grades Mathematics Instruction." *Journal for Research in Mathematics Education* 44, no. 4 (2013): 646–82.

Jacobs, Victoria R., and Rebecca C. Ambrose. "Making the Most of Story Problems." *Teaching Children Mathematics* 15, no. 5 (2008): 260–66.

Jacobs, Victoria R., Lisa L. C. Lamb, and Randolph A. Philipp. "Professional Noticing of Children's Mathematical Thinking." *Journal for Research in Mathematics Education* 41, no. 2 (2010): 169–202.

Kanold, Timothy D., and Matthew R. Larson. *Common Core Mathematics in a PLC at Work: Leader's Guide.* Bloomington, Ind.: Solution Tree Press; Reston, Va.: National Council of Teachers of Mathematics, 2012.

Kapur, Manu. "Productive Failure in Mathematical Problem Solving." *Instructional Science* 38, no. 6 (2010): 523–50.

Keck, Heidi, and Johnny Lott. "Integrated Mathematics through Mathematical Modeling." In *Integrated Mathematics: Choices and Challenges*, edited by Sue Ann McGraw, pp. 131–140. Reston, Va.: National Council of Teachers of Mathematics, 2003.

Kisker, Ellen Eliason, Jerry Lipka, Barbara L. Adams, Anthony Rickard, Dora Andrew-Ihrke, Eva Evelyn Yanez, and Ann Millard. "The Potential of a Culturally-Based Supplemental Math Curriculum to Reduce the Math Performance Gap between Alaska Native and Other Students." *Journal for Research in Mathematics Education* 43, no. 1 (2012): 75–113.

Knapp, Michael S., Nancy E. Adelman, Camille Marder, Heather McCollum, Margaret C. Needels, Christine Padillia, Patrick M. Shields, Brenda J. Turnbull, and Andrew A. Zucker. *Teaching for Meaning in High-Poverty Schools.* New York: Teachers College Press, 1995.

Knight, Jim. *Instructional Coaching: A Partnership Approach to Improving Instruction.* Thousand Oaks, Calif.: Corwin, 2007.

Korthagen, Fred A. J., and Angelo Vasalos. "Going to the Core: Deepening Reflection by Connecting the Person to the Profession." In *Handbook of Reflection and Reflective Inquiry: Mapping a Way of Knowing for Professional Reflective Inquiry*, edited by Nona Lyons, pp. 529–52. New York: Springer, 2010.

Lampert, Magdalene. "Learning Teaching in, from, and for Practice: What Do We Mean?" *Journal of Teacher Education* 61, no. 1/2 (2010): 21–34.

Leahy, Siobhan, Christine Lyon, Marnie Thompson, and Dylan Wiliam. "Classroom Assessment: Minute by Minute, Day by Day." *Educational Leadership* 63, no. 3 (2005): 18–24.

Lesh, Richard, Tom Post, and Merlyn Behr. "Representations and Translations among Representations in Mathematics Learning and Problem Solving." In *Problems of Representation in the Teaching and Learning of Mathematics*, edited by Claude Janvier, pp. 33–40. Hillsdale, N.J.: Erlbaum, 1987.

Lester, Frank K., Jr., ed. *Second Handbook of Research on Mathematics Teaching and Learning.* Charlotte, N.C.: Information Age; Reston, Va.: National Council of Teachers of Mathematics, 2007.

Lewis, Catherine. *Lesson Study: A Handbook of Teacher-Led Instructional Change.* Philadelphia: Research for Better Schools, 2002.

Lipka, Jerry, Nancy Sharp, Barbara Adams, and Ferdinand Sharp. "Creating a Third Space for Authentic Biculturalism: Examples from Math in a Cultural Context." *Journal of American Indian Education* 46, no. 3 (2007): 94–115.

Lubienski, Sarah Theule. "Research, Reform and Equity in U.S. Mathematics Education." In *Improving Access to Mathematics: Diversity and Equity in the Classroom*, edited by Na'ilah Suad Nasir and Paul Cobb, pp. 10–23. New York: Teachers College Press, 2006.

Ma, Liping. *Knowing and Teaching Elementary Mathematics: Teachers' Understanding of Fundamental Mathematics in China and the United States.* 2nd ed. New York: Routledge, 2010.

Marshall, Anne Marie, Alison Castro Superfine, and Reality S. Canty. "Star Students Make Connections." *Teaching Children Mathematics* 17, no. 1 (2010): 39–47.

Martin, Danny Bernard. "Hidden Assumptions and Unaddressed Questions in Mathematics for ALL Rhetoric." *Mathematics Educator* 13, no. 2 (2003): 7–21.

Martin, W. Gary. "The NCTM High School Curriculum Project: Why It Matters to You." *Mathematics Teacher* 103, no. 3 (2009): 164–66.

Martin, W. Gary, Marilyn E. Strutchens, Stephen Stuckwisch, and Mohammed Qazi. "Transforming East Alabama Mathematics (TEAM-Math): Promoting Systemic Change in Schools and Universities." In *Disrupting Tradition: Research and Practice Pathways in Mathematics Education*, edited by William F. Tate, Karen D. King, and Celia Rousseau Anderson, pp. 105–18. Reston, Va.: National Council of Teachers of Mathematics, 2011.

Marzano, Robert J. *What Works in Schools: Translating Research into Action.* Alexandria, Va.: Association of Supervision and Curriculum Development, 2003.

———. *Designing and Teaching Learning Goals and Objectives: Classroom Strategies That Work.* Bloomington, Ind.: Marzano Research Laboratory, 2009.

Marzano, Robert J., Tina Boogren, Tammy Heflebower, Jessica Kanold-McIntyre, and Debra Pickering. *Becoming a Reflective Teacher.* Bloomington, Ind.: Marzano Research Laboratory, 2012.

Mathematical Sciences Research Institute (MSRI). *Teaching Teachers Mathematics: Research, Ideas, Projects, Evaluation.* Cathy Kessel, ed. Critical Issues in Mathematics Education, vol. 3. Berkeley, Calif.: MSRI, 2009.

Mayer, Richard E. "Rote versus Meaningful Learning." *Theory into Practice* 41, no. 4 (2002): 226–32.

McDonald, Morva, Elham Kazemi, and Sarah Schneider Kavanagh. "Core Practices and Pedagogies of Teacher Education: A Call for a Common Language and Collective Activity." *Journal of Teacher Education* 64, no. 5 (2013): 378–86.

McGatha, Maggie. *Mathematics Specialists and Mathematics Coaches: What Does the Research Say?* NCTM Research Brief. Reston, Va.: National Council of Teachers of Mathematics, 2009.

McKenzie, Kathryn Bell, Linda Skrla, James Joseph Scheurich, Delores Rice, and Daniel P. Hawes. "Math and Science Academic Success in Three Large, Diverse, Urban High Schools: A Teachers' Story." *Journal of Education for Students Placed at Risk* 16, no. 2 (2011): 100–21.

McTighe, Jay, and Grant P. Wiggins. *Essential Questions: Opening Doors to Student Understanding.* Alexandria, Va.: Association for Supervision and Curriculum Development, 2013.

Mehan, Hugh. *Learning Lessons: Social Organization in the Classroom.* Cambridge, Mass.: Harvard University Press, 1979.

Michaels, Sarah, Mary Catherine O'Connor, and Lauren Resnick. "Deliberative Discourse Idealized and Realized: Accountable Talk in the Classroom and in Civic Life." *Studies in Philosophy and Education* 27, no. 4 (2008): 283–97.

Middleton, James A., and Amanda Jansen. *Motivation Matters and Interest Counts: Fostering Engagement in Mathematics.* Reston, Va.: National Council of Teachers of Mathematics, 2011.

Moller, Stephanie, Roslyn Arlin Mickelson, Elizabeth Stearns, Neena Banerjee, and Martha Cecilia Bottia. "Collective Pedagogical Teacher Culture and Mathematics Achievement Differences by Race, Ethnicity, and Socioeconomic Status." *Sociology of Education* 86, no. 2 (2013): 174–94.

Morris, Anne K., James Hiebert, and Sandy M. Spitzer. "Mathematical Knowledge for Teaching in Planning and Evaluating Instruction: What Can Preservice Teachers Learn?" *Journal for Research in Mathematics Education* 40, no. 5 (2009): 491–29.

Moschkovich, Judit N. "Understanding the Needs of Latino Students in Reform-Oriented Mathematics Classrooms." In *Changing the Faces of Mathematics: Perspectives on Latinos*, edited by Luis Ortiz-Franco, Norma G. Hernández, and Yolanda de la Cruz, pp. 5–12. Reston, Va.: National Council of Teachers of Mathematics, 1999.

———. "Supporting Mathematical Reasoning and Sense Making for English Learners." In *Focus in High School Mathematics: Fostering Reasoning and Sense Making for All Students*, edited by Marilyn E. Strutchens and Judith Reed Quander, pp. 17–36. Reston, Va.: NCTM, 2011.

National Center for Education Statistics (NCES). *NAEP 2008: Trends in Academic Progress.* NCES 2009–479. Washington, D.C.: NCES, 2009.

———. *A First Look: 2013 Mathematics and Reading.* NCES 2014-451. Washington, D.C.: NCES, 2013.

———. Reports generated by using the NAEP Data Explorer. Washington, D.C.: NCES, 2014. http://nces.ed.gov/nationsreportcard/naepdata/.

National Center on Education and the Economy (NCEE) and the University of Pittsburgh. *New Standards Performance Standards: English Language Arts, Mathematics, Science, Applied Learning,* Vol. 2, *Middle School.* Washington, D.C.: NCEE; Pittsburgh, Pa.: University of Pittsburgh, 1997.

National Council of Teachers of Mathematics (NCTM). *Curriculum and Evaluation Standards for School Mathematics.* Reston, Va.: NCTM, 1989.

————. *Professional Standards for Teaching Mathematics.* Reston, Va.: NCTM, 1991.

————. *Assessment Standards for School Mathematics.* Reston, Va.: NCTM, 1995.

————. *Principles and Standards for School Mathematics.* Reston, Va.: NCTM, 2000.

————. *Mathematics Teaching Today: Improving Practice, Improving Student Learning,* 2nd ed. Updated, revised version of *Professional Standards for Teaching Mathematics* (NCTM 1991), edited by Tami S. Martin. Reston, Va.: NCTM, 2007.

————. *Focus in High School Mathematics: Reasoning and Sense Making.* Reston, Va.: NCTM, 2009.

————. *Technology in Teaching and Learning Mathematics.* NCTM Position Statement, 2011. http://www.nctm.org/about/content.aspx?id=6330.

————. *Supporting the Common Core State Standards for Mathematics.* NCTM Position Statement, 2013. http://www.nctm.org/ccssmposition.

National Governors Association Center for Best Practices and Council of Chief State School Officers (NGA Center and CCSSO). *Common Core State Standards for Mathematics. Common Core State Standards (College- and Career-Readiness Standards and K–12 Standards in English Language Arts and Math).* Washington, D.C.: NGA Center and CCSSO, 2010. http://www.corestandards.org.

————. *K–8 Publishers' Criteria for the Common Core State Standards for Mathematics.* Washington, D.C.: NGA Center and CCSSO, 2013. http://www.corestandards.org /assets/Math_Publishers_Criteria_K-8_Summer%202012_FINAL.pdf.

National Mathematics Advisory Panel (NMAP). *Foundations for Success: The Final Report of the National Mathematics Advisory Panel.* Washington, D.C.: U.S. Department of Education, 2008.

National Research Council. *Adding It Up: Helping Children Learn Mathematics.* Jeremy Kilpatrick, Jane Swafford, and Bradford Findell, eds., Mathematics Learning Study Committee, Center for Education, Division of Behavioral and Social Sciences and Education. Washington, D.C.: National Academy Press, 2001.

————. *Mathematics Learning in Early Childhood: Paths toward Excellence and Equity.* Christopher T. Cross, Taniesha A. Woods, and Heidi Schweingruber, eds., Committee on Early Childhood Mathematics, Center for Education, Division of Behavioral and Social Sciences and Education. Washington, D.C.: National Academies Press, 2009.

———. *Education for Life and Work: Developing Transferable Knowledge and Skills in the 21st Century.* James W. Pellegrino and Margaret L. Hilton, eds., Committee on Defining Deeper Learning and 21st Century Skills, Board on Testing and Assessment and Board on Science Education, Division of Behavioral and Social Sciences and Education. Washington, D.C.: National Academies Press, 2012a.

———. *A Framework for K–12 Science Education: Practices, Crosscutting Concepts, and Core Ideas.* Washington, D.C.: National Academies Press, 2012b.

———. *The Mathematical Sciences in 2025.* Washington, D.C.: National Academies Press, 2013a.

———. *Next Generation Science Standards: For States, by States.* Washington, D.C.: National Academies Press, 2013b.

Organisation for Economic Co-operation and Development (OECD). *Lessons from PISA 2012 for the United States, Strong Performers and Successful Reformers in Education.* Paris: OECD, 2013b. http://dx.doi.org/10.1787/9789264207585-en.

———. *PISA 2012 Results in Focus: What 15-Year-Olds Know and What They Can Do with What They Know.* Paris: OECD, 2013a.

Orlich, Donald C. "Education Reform and Limits to Student Achievement." *Phi Delta Kappan* 81, no. 6 (2000): 468–72.

Otto, Albert Dean, Janet H. Caldwell, Cheryl Ann Lubinski, and Sarah Wallus Hancock. *Developing Essential Understanding of Multiplication and Division for Teaching Mathematics in Grades 3–5.* Essential Understanding Series. Reston, Va.: NCTM, 2011.

Pape, Stephen J., and Mourat A. Tchoshanov. "The Role of Representation(s) in Developing Mathematical Understanding." *Theory into Practice* 40, no. 2 (2001): 118–27.

Partnership for Assessment of Readiness for College and Careers (PARCC). TV Sales prototype task, 2013. http://www.ccsstoolbox.com/parcc/PARCCPrototype_main.html.

Pashler, Harold, Patrice M. Bain, Brian A. Bottge, Arthur Graesser, Kenneth Koedinger, Mark McDaniel, and Janet Metcalfe. *Organizing Instruction and Study to Improve Student Learning.* IES Practice Guide (NCER 2007-2004). Washington, D.C.: National Center for Education Research, Institute of Education Sciences, U.S. Department of Education, 2007. http://ncer.ed.gov.

Perry, Angela. *The Data Teams Experience: A Guide for Effective Meetings.* Englewood, Colo.: Advanced Learning Press, 2011.

Phelps, Geoffrey, Douglas Corey, Jenny DeMonte, Delena Harrison, and Deborah Loewenberg Ball. "How Much English Language Arts and Mathematics Instruction Do Students Receive? Investigating Variation in Instructional Time." *Educational Policy* 26, no. 5 (2012): 631–62.

Philipp, Randolph A. "Mathematics Teachers' Beliefs and Affect." In *Second Handbook of Research on Mathematics Teaching and Learning*, edited by Frank K. Lester, Jr., pp. 257–315. Charlotte, N.C.: Information Age; Reston, Va.: National Council of Teachers of Mathematics, 2007.

Planas, Núria, and Marta Civil. "Language-as-Resource and Language-as-Political: Tensions in the Bilingual Mathematics Classroom." *Mathematics Education Research Journal* 25, no. 3 (2013): 361–78.

Popham, W. James. *Transformative Assessment.* Alexandria, Va.: Association for Supervision and Curriculum Development, 2008.

Ramirez, Gerardo, Elizabeth A. Gunderson, Susan C. Levine, and Sian L. Beilock. "Math Anxiety, Working Memory, and Math Achievement in Early Elementary School." *Journal of Cognition and Development* 14, no. 2 (2013): 187–202.

Rathmell, Edward C. *Basic Facts: Questions, Answers, and Comments.* Cedar Falls, Iowa: Thinking with Numbers, 2005. http://www.thinkingwithnumbers.com.

Razfar, Aria, Lena Lecón Khisty, and Kathryn Chval. (2011). "Re-mediating Second Language Acquisition: A Socioculutural Perspective for Language Development." *Mind, Culture, and Activity* 18, no. 3: 195–215.

Reeves, Douglas B. *Elements of Grading: A Guide to Effective Practices.* Bloomington, Ind.: Solution Tree Press, 2011.

Reinhart, Steven C. "Never Say Anything a Kid Can Say!" *Mathematics Teaching in the Middle School* 5, no. 8 (2000): 478–83.

Robinson, Keith. "Early Disparities in Mathematics Gains among Poor and Non-Poor Children." *Elementary School Journal* 114, no. 1 (2013): 22–47.

Rohrer, Doug. "The Effects of Spacing and Mixed Practice Problems." *Journal for Research in Mathematics Education* 40, no. 1 (2009): 4–17.

Rohrer, Doug, and Kelli Taylor. "The Shuffling of Mathematics Problems Improves Learning." *Instructional Science* 35, no. 6 (2007): 481–98.

Ronau, Robert N., Christopher R. Rakes, Sarah B. Bush, Shannon Driskell, Margaret L. Niess, and David Pugalee. *Using Calculators for Teaching and Learning Mathematics.* NCTM Research Brief. Reston, Va.: National Council of Teachers of Mathematics, 2000. http://www.nctm.org/news/content.aspx?id=8468.

Roschelle, Jeremy, Nicole Shechtman, Deborah Tatar, Stephen Hegedus, Bill Hopkins, Susan Empson, Jennifer Knudsen, and Lawrence P. Gallagher. "Integration of Technology, Curriculum, and Professional Development for Advancing Middle School Mathematics: Three Large-Scale Studies." *American Educational Research Journal* 47, no. 4 (2010): 833–78.

Rubin, Beth C., and Pedro A. Noguera. "Tracking Detracking: Sorting through the Dilemmas and Possibilities of Detracking in Practice." *Equity and Excellence in Education* 37, no. 1 (2004): 92–101.

Russell, Susan Jo. "Developing Computational Fluency with Whole Numbers." *Teaching Children Mathematics* 7, no. 3 (2000): 154–58.

Sam, Lim Chap, and Paul Ernest. "A Survey of Public Images of Mathematics." *Research in Mathematics Education* 2, no. 1 (2000): 193–206.

Sarama, Julie, and Douglas H. Clements. "'Concrete' Computer Manipulatives in Mathematics Education." *Child Development Perspectives* 3, no. 3 (2009): 145–50.

Schifter, Deborah. "Learning to See the Invisible: What Skills and Knowledge Are Needed to Engage with Students' Mathematical Ideas?" In *Beyond Classical Pedagogy: Teaching Elementary School Mathematics*, edited by Terry Wood, Barbara S. Nelson, and Janet Warfield, pp. 109–34. Mahwah, N.J.: Erlbaum, 2001.

Schmidt, William H., Leland S. Cogan, and Richard T. Houang. "Equality of Educational Opportunity: Myth or Reality in U.S. Schooling?" *American Educator* 34, no. 4 (2011): pp. 12–19.

Schmidt, William H., Richard T. Houang, and Leland S. Cogan. "A Coherent Curriculum: The Case of Mathematics." *American Educator* 26, no. 2 (2002): 10–26; 47–48.

Schmoker, Michael J. *Results Now: How We Can Achieve Unprecedented Improvements in Teaching and Learning.* Alexandria, Va.: Association for Supervision and Curriculum Development, 2006.

Scholastic and the Bill & Melinda Gates Foundation. *Primary Sources: 2012—America's Teachers on the Teaching Profession.* New York: Scholastic, 2012.

Schunk, Dale H., and Kerry Richardson. "Motivation and Self-Efficacy in Mathematics Education." In *Motivation and Disposition: Pathways to Learning Mathematics*, edited by Daniel J. Brahier, pp. 13–30. Reston, Va.: National Council of Teachers of Mathematics, 2011.

Seeley, Cathy L. *Faster Isn't Smarter: Messages about Math, Teaching, and Learning in the 21st Century.* Sausalito, Calif.: Math Solutions, 2009.

Seidle, Tina, Rolf Rimmele, and Manfred Prenzel. "Clarity and Coherence of Lesson Goals as a Scaffold for Student Learning." *Learning and Instruction* 15, no. 6 (2005): 539–56.

Sherin, Miriam Gamoran, and Elizabeth A. van Es. "A New Lens on Teaching: Learning to Notice." *Mathematics Teaching in the Middle School* 9, no. 2 (2003): 92–95.

Sleep, Laurie, and Timothy A. Boerst. "Preparing Beginning Teachers to Elicit and Interpret Students' Mathematical Thinking." *Teaching and Teacher Education* 28, no. 7 (2012): 1038–48.

Smith, Margaret S. "Reflections on Practice: Redefining Success in Mathematics Teaching and Learning." *Mathematics Teaching in the Middle School* 5, no. 6 (2000): 378–82, 386.

Smith, Margaret S., Edward A. Silver, Mary Kay Stein, Melissa Boston, and Marjorie A. Henningsen. *Improving Instruction in Rational Numbers and Proportionality: Using Cases to Transform Mathematics Teaching and Learning.* Vol. 1. New York: Teachers College Press, 2005.

Smith, Margaret S., and Mary Kay Stein. *5 Practices for Orchestrating Productive Mathematics Discussions.* Reston, Va.: National Council of Teachers of Mathematics, 2011.

————. "Selecting and Creating Mathematical Tasks: From Research to Practice." *Mathematics Teaching in the Middle School* 3, no. 5 (1998): 344–49.

Staples, Megan E. "Promoting Student Collaboration in a Detracked, Heterogeneous Secondary Mathematics Classroom." *Journal of Mathematics Teacher Education* 11, no. 5 (2008): 349–71.

Stein, Mary Kay, Barbara W. Grover, and Marjorie Henningsen. "Building Student Capacity for Mathematical Thinking and Reasoning: An Analysis of Mathematical Tasks Used in Reform Classrooms." *American Educational Research Journal* 33, no. 2 (1996): 455–88.

Stein, Mary Kay, and Suzanne Lane. "Instructional Tasks and the Development of Student Capacity to Think and Reason: An Analysis of the Relationship between Teaching and Learning in a Reform Mathematics Project." *Educational Research and Evaluation* 2, no. 1 (1996): 50-80.

Stein, Mary K., Janine Remillard, and Margaret S. Smith. "How Curriculum Influences Student Learning." In *Second Handbook of Research on Mathematics Teaching and Learning,* edited by Frank K. Lester, Jr., pp. 319–69. Charlotte, N.C.: Information Age; Reston, Va.: National Council of Teachers of Mathematics, 2007.

Stein, Mary Kay, Jennifer Russell, and Margaret Schwan Smith. "The Role of Tools in Bridging Research and Practice in an Instructional Improvement Effort." In *Disrupting Tradition: Research and Practice Pathways in Mathematics Education,* edited by William F. Tate, Karen D. King, and Celia Rousseau Anderson, pp. 33–44. Reston, Va.: National Council of Teachers of Mathematics, 2011.

Stein, Mary Kay, and Margaret S. Smith. "Mathematical Tasks as a Framework for Reflection: From Research to Practice." *Mathematics Teaching in the Middle School* 3, no. 4 (1998): 268–75.

Stein, Mary Kay, Margaret S. Smith, Marjorie Henningsen, and Edward A. Silver. *Implementing Standards-Based Mathematics Instruction: A Casebook for Professional Development.* 2nd ed. New York: Teachers College Press, 2009.

Stiff, Lee V., Janet L. Johnson, and Patrick Akos. "Examining What We Know for Sure: Tracking in Middle Grades Mathematics." In *Disrupting Tradition: Research and Practice Pathways in Mathematics Education,* edited by William Tate, Karen King, and Celia Rousseau Anderson, pp. 63–75. Reston, Va.: National Council of Teachers of Mathematics, 2011.

Stiggins, Rick. "Assessment through the Student's Eyes." *Educating the Whole Child* 64, no. 8 (2007): 22–26.

Stigler, James W., and James Hiebert. *The Teaching Gap: Best Ideas from the World's Teachers for Improving Education in the Classroom.* New York: Simon and Schuster, 1999.

———. "Improving Mathematics Teaching." *Educational Leadership* 61, no. 5 (2004): 12–16.

Stigler, James W., and Belinda J. Thompson. "Thoughts on Creating, Accumulating, and Utilizing Shareable Knowledge to Improve Teaching." *Elementary School Journal* 109, no. 5 (2009): 442–57.

Stylianou, Despina A., and Edward A. Silver. "The Role of Visual Representations in Advanced Mathematical Problem Solving: An Examination of Expert-Novice Similarities and Differences." *Mathematical Thinking and Learning* 6, no. 4 (2004): 353–87.

Swan, Malcolm. "Dealing with Misconceptions in Mathematics." In *Issues in Mathematics Teaching*, edited by Peter Gates, pp. 147–65. New York: Routledge, 2001.

Sztajn, Paola, Jere Confrey, P. Holt Wilson, and Cynthia Edgington. "Learning Trajectory Based Instruction: Toward a Theory of Teaching." *Educational Researcher* 41, no. 5 (2012): 147–56.

Tarr, James E., Óscar Chávez, Robert E. Reys, and Barbara J. Reys. "From the Written to the Enacted Curricula: The Intermediary Role of Middle School Mathematics Teachers in Shaping Students' Opportunity to Learn." *School Science and Mathematics* 106, no. 4 (2006): 191–201.

Tate, William F., and Celia Rousseau. "Access and Opportunity: The Political and Social Context of Mathematics Education." In *Handbook of International Research in Mathematics Education*, edited by Lyn D. English, pp. 271–99. Mahwah, N.J.: Erlbaum, 2002.

Thornton, Carol A. "Emphasizing Thinking Strategies in Basic Fact Instruction." *Journal for Research in Mathematics Education* (1978): 214–27.

Tripathi, Preety N. "Developing Mathematical Understanding through Multiple Representations." *Mathematics Teaching in the Middle School* 13, no. 8 (2008): 438–45.

U.S. Department of Education (ED). *Science, Technology, Engineering and Math: Education for Global Leadership.* Washington, D.C.: ED, 2014. http://www.ed.gov/stem.

van Es, Elizabeth A. "A Framework for Learning to Notice Student Thinking." In *Mathematics Teacher Noticing: Seeing through Teachers' Eyes*, edited by Miriam Gamoran Sherin, Victoria R. Jacobs, and Randolph A. Philipp, pp. 134–51. New York: Routledge, 2010.

Wager, Anita A. "Incorporating Out-of-School Mathematics: From Cultural Context to Embedded Practice." *Journal of Mathematics Teacher Education* 15, no. 1 (2012): 9–23.

Walker, Erica N. (2003). "Who Can Do Mathematics?" In *Activating Mathematical Talent*, edited by Bruce R. Vogeli and Alexander Karp, pp. 15–27. Boston: Houghton Mifflin and National Council of Supervisors of Mathematics, 2003.

Walsh, Jackie Acree, and Beth Dankert Sattes. *Quality Questioning: Research-Based Practice to Engage Every Learner*. Thousand Hills, Calif.: Corwin Press, 2005.

Warshauer, Hiroko Kawaguchi. "The Role of Productive Struggle in Teaching and Learning Middle School Mathematics." PhD diss., University of Texas at Austin, 2011.

Webb, David C., Nina Boswinkel, and Truus Dekker. "Beneath the Tip of the Iceberg: Using Representations to Support Student Understanding." *Mathematics Teaching in the Middle School* 14, no. 2 (2008): 110–13.

Webel, Corey. "Shifting Mathematical Authority from Teacher to Community." *Mathematics Teacher* 104, no. 4 (2010): 315–18.

Wei, Ruth Chung, Linda Darling-Hammond, Alethea Andree, Nikole Richardson, and Stelios Orphanos. *Professional Learning in the Learning Profession: A Status Report on Teacher Development in the United States and Abroad*. Dallas, Tex.: National Staff Development Council, 2009.

Weiss, Iris R., and Joan D. Pasley. "What Is High-Quality Instruction?" *Educational Leadership* 61, no. 5 (2004): 24–28.

White, Stephen H. *Beyond the Numbers: Making Data Work for Teachers and School Leaders*. Englewood, Colo.: Advanced Learning Press, 2011.

Wiggins, Grant, and Jay McTighe. *Understanding by Design*. Alexandria, Va.: Association for Supervision and Curriculum Development, 1998.

Wiliam, Dylan. "Content *Then* Process: Teacher Learning Communities in the Service of Formative Assessment." In *Ahead of the Curve: The Power of Assessment to Transform Teaching and Learning*, edited by Douglas Reeves, pp. 183–204. Bloomington, Ind.: Solution Tree Press, 2007b.

———. "Keeping Learning on Track: Classroom Assessment and the Regulation of Learning." In *Second Handbook of Mathematics Teaching and Learning*, edited by Frank K. Lester, Jr., pp. 1053–98. Charlotte, N.C.: Information Age; Reston, Va.: National Council of Teachers of Mathematics, 2007a.

———. *Embedded Formative Assessment*. Bloomington, Ind.: Solution Tree Press, 2011.

Wilkins, Jesse L. M. "The Relationship among Elementary Teachers' Content Knowledge, Attitudes, Beliefs, and Practices." *Journal of Mathematics Teacher Education* 11, no. 2 (2008): 139–64.

Williams, Belinda. "Reframing the Reform Agenda." In *Closing the Achievement Gaps: A Vision for Changing Beliefs and Practices*, edited by Belinda Williams, pp. 178–96, Alexandria, Va.: Association for Supervision and Curriculum Development, 2003.

Wood, Terry. "Alternative Patterns of Communication in Mathematics Classes: Funneling or Focusing?" In *Language and Communication in the Mathematics Classroom*, edited by Heinz Steinbring, Maria G. Bartolini Bussi, and Anna Sierpinska, pp. 167–78. Reston, Va.: National Council of Teachers of Mathematics, 1998.

Wood, Terry, and Tammy Turner-Vorbeck. "Extending the Conception of Mathematics Teaching." In *Beyond Classical Pedagogy: Teaching Elementary School Mathematics*, edited by Terry Wood, Barbara Scott Nelson, and Janet Warfield, pp. 185–208. Mahwah, N.J.: Erlbaum, 2001.

Zimba, Jason. "Examples of Structure in the *Common Core State Standards*' Standards for Mathematical Content" (draft, 2011). http://ime.math.arizona.edu/2011-12 /ccssatlas_2011_07_06_0956_p1p2.pdf.

Zimmerman, Barry J. "Theories of Self-Regulated Learning and Academic Achievement: An Overview and Analysis." In *Self-Regulated Learning and Academic Achievement: Theoretical Perspectives*, edited by Barry J. Zimmerman and Dale H. Schunk, pp. 1–65. Mahwah, N.J.: Erlbaum, 2001.